LOVE
never dies

JANE DE FOREST

ILLUSTRATED BY JANE DE FOREST & TARA DE FOREST

www.janesinspiration.com

Jane's Inspiration Press

JANE'S INSPIRATION, LLC
Regarding: Jane de Forest
Box 499
Camas, WA 98607

LOVE NEVER DIES. A PSYCHIC ARTIST ILLUSTRATES TRUE STORIES OF THE AFTERLIFE
FIRST EDITION

ILLUSTRATIONS BY JANE DE FOREST AND TARA DE FOREST

ISBN 978-1-947-369-01-6

To my family

CONTENTS

ACKNOWLEDGEMENTS

FIRST, I WOULD LIKE TO thank those who have momentarily slipped my mind but not my heart and the brave people who allowed me to tell their stories. . . thank you.

This book would only be an idea, had I not invited my mother, Mariah Imberman de Forest, to come live with us. She did an amazing job editing my manuscript. Without her help, this book would not have been possible. Thank you to Katrina and Sophia for making my heart smile always and to my husband, Christopher, who is my greatest fan and positive force, encouraging me unceasingly. To my amazing daughter, Tara, who did the lion's share of illustrations. Thank you to all the other two and four-legged friends who depend on me. Linda, my patient, brilliant and generous publisher, who is now a friend. Thanks to the New Renaissance Bookshop, the new-thought hub in the Northwest U.S. and its owners, Darlene, Jamey and Claire—I am so grateful to work with such kind, evolved, and visionary people. It is my favorite place to do intuitive coaching and readings and teach in Portland, OR.

I want to also recognize wise bee goddess, Susan, who wrote a lovely introduction and is a founding member of "Writers of The Purple Sage", the writers' group that met weekly at the library, and to Pixie, also a founding member, who has brightened my life, blessed my heart and inspired me for many years. I am so grateful to Jim, a guitarist who played with the Grateful Dead, for showing up so well. Thank you to Abby, I love you, and to my Munda, I miss you lots. I am deeply grateful to Woody for his thoughtful insights and advice even when he was ill, I love you lots. I appreciate deeply my mother-in-law, beautiful Eve, and Bob. Thank you to those in my family who I love with all my heart, and who make the world a better place.

Thank you to my friends for all your sweetness, support and loyal hearts. Thank you.

To my ancestors, guides, angels and all those souls on the other side who try so hard to get through to me and make my job the best job in the whole world, my deepest heartfelt gratitude.

Finally, thank you to those who inspired me: Ingo Swann, Uri Geller, Jane Goodall, Jean Houston, Sarah Harris, Graham Hancock, George Noory, Carmen Bolter, Michael Newton, Nasim Harimine, Gregg Braden, Dean Raden, Louise Hay, Louise Hauck, Joseph Campbell, Eben Alexander, Erich von Daniken, Joe Dispenza, Stan Groff, Richard Alpert aka Ram Dass, Elisabeth Kübler-Ross, Dalai Lama, Joan Boresanko, Joe McMoneagle, Shafica Karagulla, Bruce Lipton, Rita Dove, Raymond Moody, Mona Lisa Scultz, Rupert Sheldrake, Huston Smith, Russell Targ, James Van Praagh, Alan Watts, Brian Weiss, oh, and The Big Guy aka, unending-loving-conscious universe.

© JANE DE FOREST

THE LESSON

INTRODUCTION

© TARA DE FOREST

INTRODUCTION

BY

SUSAN CHERNAK McELROY

Author of the New York Times bestseller
Animals as Teacher and Guides for the Soul,
and
All My Relations Living with Animals as Teachers and Healers

JANE IS A RARE BIRD. That she is wildly creative in a multitude of venues is amazing enough, but she brings unique qualities to her creative life that make her—in my book—a endangered species. As an artist myself, I fully relate to the stereotype of creatives as overly-emotional, moody, and—how shall I say this—airy-fairy.

Creative types are commonly known to have both feet wading in the clouds much of the time. From personal experience, I have to say this is true. I spend a considerable amount of time sitting with eyes unfocused, pondering imaginary realms and lofty possibilities. At times, in the midst of a creative wave, it is hard for me to get back to the beach.

But Jane, who is able to travel gracefully between dimensions of time and space, has her feet firmly planted on the ground. She is an artist and medium of enormous, raw talent who is rooted in a base of practicality, humility, and humor that I find refreshing, amusing, and profoundly comforting.

When Jane asked if I would write the introduction to her book, I told her I wanted to have a reading with her about my mother, so I could speak from fresh experience. My mother died six months ago in my house while on hospice care and I have been pondering her passing and wondering how her spirit is doing. So on a sunny spring day, Jane and I sat down with tumblers full of rosemary-lemon water on her deck overlooking the green-carpeted hills of Western Washington, preparing to visit with Minnie.

Jane knew only that Minnie had died in our house and that my mother and I had not had the easiest of relationships. On the table with our water glasses was a sketch pad and pencil and her phone to record. Inside the house, Jane's paintings lined the walls. Balinese umbrellas hung from the ceiling with dangling twinkly lights in an imitation of soft Northwest rain.

Just the right amount of other-worldliness, I thought, just the right amount to let a person know that mystery and whimsy abide in Jane's place.

As we settled into the cushy deck chairs, I thought about the many intuitive readings I'd had in my life, mostly when I was considerably younger. There was a time when I trusted myself very little, trusting instead the guidance of intuitives, mediums, and psychics to help me chart the course of my life. I got a lot of good information during those days and stopped scheduling sessions only because I grew a greater faith in myself and my ability to steer my own course. Still, there are times when it is nearly impossible for me to get enough distance from a problem to see it clearly, especially when the problem is a person, a relationship. In such cases, a good intuitive reading can be worth a year of heavy counseling. Trust me on this. My behind has seen its share of counselors' sofas.

It occurred to me, sitting in the sun on that lovely day, that what I look for in an intuitive is actually the same thing I look for in a good counselor: someone who is gifted, who is passionate about the work, and who makes me feel safe. It is not easy to open up the most intimate details of your life to another person. Far more important to me than testimonials and degrees is that I have a deep feeling of safety before any of the work begins. Safety first, Minnie always said.

Jane's intuitive gifts are amazing, yet it is the sense of safe-harbor, authenticity, and feet-on-the-ground sensibility that she brings to her life and her readings that make me cherish her. I knew Minnie and I were in good hands that afternoon.

The session began with Jane "checking in" to see if we could find Minnie. Along the way, she would share impressions she was getting as she established contact with my mother. "I need to be at least eighty percent correct in my information to be certain for myself that whom I'm speaking with is really Minnie," Jane said. Her hands worked at the sketchpad, drawing symbols and a small portrait of my mother. Jane clicked off a list of facts, all of them correct details from my mother's life.

"I think we have her here, don't you?" Jane queried.

"Yes, that would be Minnie," I laughed.

"Minnie is showing me that at some time in her life she had the opportunity to fly, but she didn't take it. She made herself small and held herself back on purpose," Jane told me. "Does that sound right to you? I'm not clear if she means literally flying or not, although I'm seeing a plane."

"No, not literally," I replied. "In her twenties, she was offered a career with EF Hutton in New York, where she was payroll manager. They wanted her to grow with the company. She said she really just wanted to be a mother, and left. After that, she did indeed become small. Her life was her yard and we two kids. I always thought it was too small for her. She lived through my brother and me and our accomplishments, and was constantly anxious and disappointed with life."

The session continued with Jane speaking for Minnie, and Minnie apologizing for what her smallness and frustration had done to our family. Minnie could see her mistakes clearly now, Jane said, and was contrite and sorry.

Jane could not know that I needed to hear that apology. Since Minnie's death, I had been carrying a lot of anger at the misery she ladled on my brother and me, especially in her later years. Minnie had been a glass-half-empty kind of gal all her life. So in her view, my brother and I were half-empty as well, never quite measuring up. Jane shared more about Minnie's new understanding of her Earth life, and of the things that had been her successes and her failures.

"Minnie wants to know if you can forgive her, even just a little bit." Jane's eyes met mine. "She says your anger hurts her on the other side and delays the healing she so needs to do for herself and for all of you."

I caught my breath. Finally, I sighed a deep breath of release. "Yes, I will begin forgiving her. I will begin it right here, today. It will take time, but it will start today."

We continued to speak a while longer, but I had almost stopped listening after Jane had said the word "forgiveness." I knew that would be the nugget of gold I would take from our session. When I left Jane's house that afternoon I left with a great deal to ponder. My tarnished relationship with Minnie had gotten a tiny bit of polishing. I had much more work to do, but Jane's words had brought me a deep measure of peace. No earthly price can be put on such a thing.

In lieu of sitting across the table from the wonder that is Jane, this book in your hands will almost—not quite, but almost—suffice. It is a wonder in itself, and a doorway into other realms that brush alongside us unseen every day. And it is also oodles of fun to read, because Jane is an interesting gal. This book is not only a tour guide to Jane's unseen dimensions, but to this real world of dirt and flowers and feasts where our feet must remain confidently planted until we release our tethers and fly.

Jane could not write a book that was just about intuitive work, because Jane is so much more than just her intuitive work, so in these pages you will find recipes, trip suggestions, art projects, guided meditations and more, to guide you gently, confidently, and happily along your way.

And when you have finished reading, and you find that even this delicious banquet of words, encouragement, insights, and inspiration is not enough to fill you, perhaps you, too, will someday find yourself sitting with a tumbler of rosemary-lemon water on a deck overlooking Mt. St. Helens, listening intently and oh-so-gratefully to Jane's messages from across the veil. I must tell you, it is a perfect place to be.

Susan Chernak McElroy

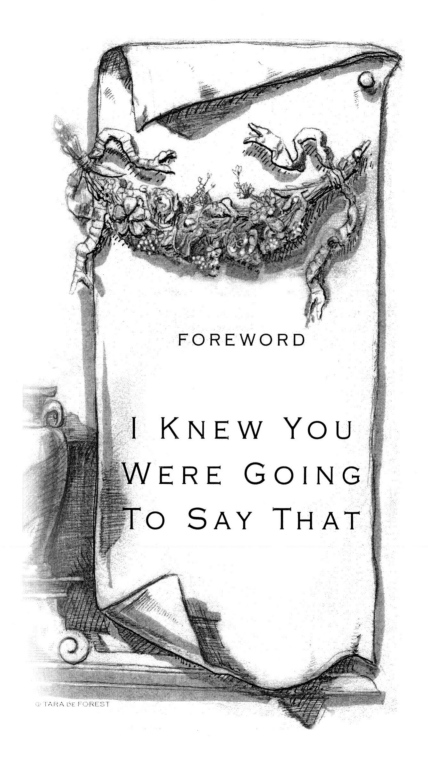

FOREWORD

I KNEW YOU WERE GOING TO SAY THAT

I KNEW YOU WERE GOING TO SAY THAT

We must let go of the life we have planned,
so as to accept the one that is waiting for us.

JOSEPH CAMPBELL

GETTING UNSTUCK

SOMETIMES WHAT PEOPLE NEED IS to get back on track and shift their thinking. This contributes to a good portion of my work—and it is a privilege and blessing to be allowed to witness the exquisite inner power, wisdom and light of fellow travelers on life's path. People are truly beautiful inside. It's not unusual for tears to flow when pent-up emotions, held back for months, years or even decades, float to the surface. Some troubled souls gain compassion from understanding a betrayer's or abuser's perspective. Many rediscover the freedom and strength to take back the parts of themselves strewn across the battlefield of life. Life can be so hard, but we don't need to struggle through by willpower alone—we have valuable tools of insight and intuition available for the asking.

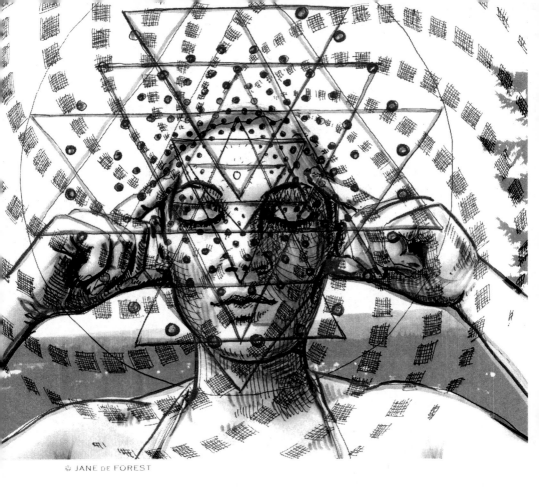

© JANE de FOREST

MIND WAVE

You have a much greater effect on the world around you
than you could ever imagine. In my intuitive consultations
with clients, I have witnessed time and time again that when
people shift their thinking, they shift their reality in that
moment. Merely perceiving reality as dimensional instead
of flat, like a 1970's disco ball (I remember them well), people
can viscerally understand there are many sides to a story.
The "story" many people tell themselves about their reality
is true, but it is only the truth from one vantage point. There
are usually plenty of other people who have a completely
different version of that same "story." When people shift their

thinking, I perceive the block in their energy field melts away in an instant. Healing happens in real time in front of my mind's eye. The process is nothing less than miraculous and is the most empowering aspect of the work I do. Changing our own reality is the beginning of changing the effect we have on others and on the world.

INTUITIVE SPECTRUM DEVELOPMENT

WHEN ANCESTORS OR ANGELS, GOD or the Universe, or your own authentic self sends you a message, it is normal and natural to understand that communication. You are supposed to "get" it. All animals have instinct, from the survival directive to fight

© JANE DE FOREST

ARRIVING HOME AFTER DEATH

or run away, to the sexual receptivity in a potential mate—it is innate. You are designed with the appropriate receivers and translators to decode your own information, and this guidance is most often accurate and benevolent. It would seem the Universe favors us—yes, God is on our side! We have WAY more power as individuals than we realize and have access to information beyond that of our limited physical brain.

Awareness, the awakened consciousness, is the first step in cultivating your second sight. Sometimes the effect occurs instantaneously with a cascade of shifted perceptions, thoughts and actions. Sometimes it takes a follow-up "home-work assignment" for those who are motivated to change. Typically, I will propose a thirty-to-forty-day exercise, depending on where my client is energetically. I'm really a translator, helping people to recognize the codes and symbols unique to them, so eventually my coaching services become unnecessary. Knowledge is power. Self-empowerment naturally arises when people choose to open their minds and hearts to the symbolic communication of an alive universe.

Most people are not interested in hearing exotic theory, but would rather use their intuitive information to be in alignment with what is authentic within themselves. Sure, winning lotto tickets would be great, but what we generally want is to make better decisions, be happy and do fulfilling, life-enhancing work. People no longer want to feel empty and live lives without meaning. A good percentage of my clientele is interested in developing their intuitive skills. With a bit of instruction and practice, the average person can make amazing strides, not only in cultivating, but in utilizing their natural intuitive instinct. This kind of intuitive knowing makes their lives richer.

INSIDE JOB

WHEN I FIRST STARTED TEACHING sixth-sense development, my mother wondered whether I would be "training the competition" by letting the cat out of the bag. I am happy to share—my goal is to help empower people through developing their higher perception. By sharing knowledge of the power dormant within us that can be awakened, we share authentic empowerment. This is power that cannot be removed through legislation, theft or destruction. It is authentic personal magnetism and strength that can stand up to injustice and make a positive difference in the world.

We can ensure an authentic positive change by empowering ourselves first, through inner transformation. From that empowered place, we do not need to save the world, because the world will automatically shift from the inside out. My prediction is that at a certain point, when enough people realize how powerful they are and how the choices they make affect our reality, critical mass will turn the tide.

WHAT I'VE DISCOVERED
AS A PROFESSIONAL INTUITIVE

AS A PROFESSIONAL INTUITIVE, I have learned and discovered information that has been extremely helpful to both my clients and myself. Here are the top ten lessons and the primary messages from stories in my book.

1. Love never dies; the love that is shared between people and animals exists forever as a shared bond.

2. You will never die; your body is discarded like a costume when your energy-self/soul returns home.

3. You will see your loved ones and animals again.

4. Home, heaven, "the place between lives," nirvana . . . is a real place, but we cannot get there wearing our body costume. We can visit during the dreamtime, euphoric experiences, and through regular mind-body-spirit disciplines like kundalini yoga, fasting and meditation.

5. When we are home in heaven, or "the place between lives," we do something. It seems as if souls on the other side are busy . . . and love what they do.

6. Our temporary home on Earth is a type of school, albeit elementary school, where we are to learn basic lessons.

7. We choose our parents, close friends and relatives in addition to our basic life situations before we enter this life. Although we incarnate with related souls, race, gender and socio-economic status differ dramatically from lifetime to lifetime.

8. We have freewill to choose love or hatred, so nothing is predetermined. There is an actual feedback loop, sometimes called karma or "what goes around comes around."

9. It is easier to resolve conflict and let go of past hurts and resentments while on Earth. Although negative thoughts and feelings can affect our loved ones after death, we have the power to heal interpersonal relationships through the veil.

10. The untapped resource of life-force energy contained within and circling throughout the human body/mind, can be utilized. Known by a variety of names, this life-force energy can be optimized.

THE BIG PICTURE AND PICTURE DRAWING: WHAT I SEE WITH MY EYES CLOSED

SEEING AND UNDERSTANDING NON-LINEAR information is a no-brainer for me. As a classically trained artist, symbols, visions, and dreams are natural and comfortable. I use an automatic drawing technique. Drawings portray the energy field around the client as well as images floating around them. Often, I draw renderings of people who have died to this world, but have come back to visit in a session.

One of the most fascinating aspects of intuitive work is that I have the honor and privilege of seeing the authentic part of a person's consciousness, or soul. I see love, joy and people's exquisite nature that shines through in moving light, colors and shapes. I also perceive several levels of energy fields corresponding to the physical body, the mind or conscience, and emotional field. Within these levels are energy hubs at internal locations on the spine, and at a spot on the top of the head. These are known as chakras.

During a reading, I can often tell whether someone is steeped in religion or has a universal perspective of the Divine. Someone raised as a Buddhist has a completely different thought-form shape than someone with a Christian background, for example. People's thoughts are light, and take different shapes and forms depending on the person's ideology—and the light is always beautiful.

Someone who meditates typically has a spacious quality of mind, like an empty room. Mental and emotional baggage I often see as boxes on a shelf; those who have released negative "stuff" such as bitterness, resentment or judgments, have only a few boxes resting neatly on the shelf of their mind. It is not uncommon for me to see people with blocks that look like gray cloudy areas in their energy field. Most people are meeting with me because they are at a "stuck" place in their lives. It is funny, but a client may say one thing and their energy field may reveal something quite different. Sometimes seeing ourselves is the most difficult assignment of all. As an artist, I am able to sketch most of what I see with my sixth sense, and my clients love being able to take the artwork home to contemplate and refer to as the future unfolds.

Can the future be predicated? Yes. The only caveat—we have free will, so I do not see life as fated, though I see the future as potential in the form of "trends." That's good news. We have the power to influence our reality in the moment and reinvent ourselves. There is always another chance.

THIS BOOK

ON THESE PAGES I SHARE my story in the most authentic way possible, with the hope my message will help someone, somewhere, in some way. All the stories are real, as are the letters following the stories, yet in some cases I have changed names or locations, or both. Sometimes I have deleted extraneous parts or changed the order of events to create a fluid narrative. I invite you to suspend disbelief and "hold on loosely" to my words, aiming instead at the underlying feelings and concepts. I am humbly attempting to describe things in plain English that express feelings, symbols, or, heck, just define the ineffable.

I have brought together the discoveries and insights, in hopes of shedding some light on the quandary of negotiating life's terrain, or what I call "earth school." I encourage you to approach this material with an open mind and take away only what resonates. If only eighty percent fits, I encourage you to leave the twenty percent that doesn't and not trash the whole concept in its entirety. Sometimes it's not what we believe, but the ability to suspend disbelief that opens us.

My goal is to tease your mind open and gently dance with your heart, to ultimately inspire you to develop your sixth sense and get in touch with what is authentic within you. Because when you are in touch with what is authentic, you are empowered. As a result, we are all stronger. And truly the world will be a better place because of your authenticity. Please sit back and enjoy a few stories from the other side of life with fellow travelers on the path.

Namaste,

Jane de Forest

I've learned that people will forget what you said,
people will forget what you did,
but people will never forget how you made them feel.

MAYA ANGELOU

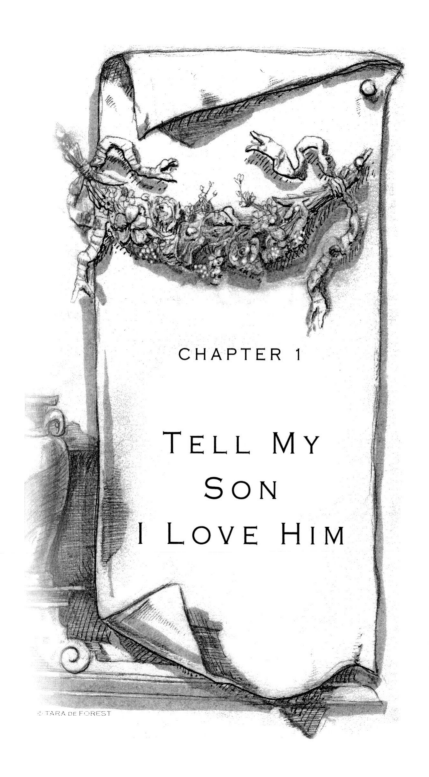

CHAPTER 1

TELL MY SON I LOVE HIM

© TARA DE FOREST

TELL MY SON
I LOVE HIM

COLE'S MOTHER, OR RATHER KARA'S SPIRIT, woke me at all hours of the night until her story was complete. The original intent was to write this down as a keepsake Cole could read when he was ready. What better than a love letter from the other side—a message of a mother's undying devotion and unconditional love for the son she'd left behind? But Cole's story grew into the book you are holding in your hands, and had this adoring mother not urgently awakened me to write the story you are about to read, this book would never have come to fruition. I am deeply grateful to Kara's family for allowing me to tell her powerful story. Most of the names and the location have not been changed.

For life and death are one,
even as the river and the sea are one.
KHALIL GIBRAN

THE AIR THUNDERED AS A Life Flight helicopter flew over the suburban subdivision in Southwest Washington. Cole was engrossed in his fifth-grade homework at the kitchen table. He instinctively got up and watched from the picture window on that sunny Mother's Day.

"Oma, come see," he called to his grandmother, Gigi.

Gigi was busy in the kitchen but she put down her towel and joined her grandson. They watched as the distinctive red helicopter moved low across the sky, from east to west. They both felt compelled to look, as it seemed to fly in slow motion.

"I've never seen a Life Flight fly that low and close to homes. Somebody must be hurt, Cole. Let's send healing energy to them." Gigi's concern for a stranger was typical of her kind heart.

Imagining love and compassion enveloping the wounded person in the helicopter, Gigi and Cole sent focused good intentions and prayers. After a few minutes, a warm, powerful flood of love and compassion washed over Gigi. It seemed as if her blessings and loving energy were being returned tenfold. That had never happened before in all the times she had sent good thoughts to people inside passing ambulances. Something was both wonderful and strange about this spring day. It seemed to her like she was living inside a dream, complete with blossoming flowers, big white puffy clouds, and the red Life Flight helicopter. But that day's dream had a surreal ending, one no one could have imagined.

Headed for the trauma unit at Emmanuel Hospital, the emergency patient inside was losing a lot of blood. Despite the paramedic's heroic efforts, her body's wounds were too severe and Kara was unable to survive.

As Gigi, Kara's mother, and Cole, Kara's son, watched Life Flight, Kara died to this world and was born to the next.

In earthly life, Kara's beautiful blond hair and penetrating blue eyes paled in comparison to her tender, kind heart. Kara was sensitive and fragile. The world was a challenging place for her,

"LOVE NEVER DIES"

cruel at times, and at other times, just too much to bare. That is when she would turn to something that could cut the pain: substances. Those times became frequent.

Kara had been in and out of rehab and her troubled life had been a source of worry for her mother. Gigi was frustrated by her inability to bring about any demonstrable positive change in her daughter's life, but she did whatever she could, and what she was doing was no small task. Without a word of discontent or complaint, she and her husband, Leif, were raising their grandson, Cole, part-time. It was "just the right thing to do," she would say. But suddenly her role with Cole became full-time.

Gigi is strong, kind, and a warm mother of four, a deeply spiritual person who is loved and cherished by friends and family. She is an environmentalist and social activist with deep concern for the plight of others less fortunate than herself. The bumper sticker on her electric car reads "Coexist," the letters created out of sacred symbols from a variety of different religions. It is how she saw the world: one love, one spirit that transcends all life.

I SETTLED IN FOR AN intuitive consultation with Gigi and was glad she had requested a reading. It was a sunny, clear September morning in the Pacific Northwest, and the warm autumn sun streamed through the burnt orange and rich purple fabric around Gigi's windows. Outside, a cross-legged Buddha sat gazing from the corner of the tidy front yard that backed onto a tree-filled ravine. Many exotic mementos from far-off lands were placed mindfully around her intimate living room.

Gigi sat quietly with me, her soft auburn waves of hair resting on her shoulders. I centered myself and said a prayer, surrounding us with the Christ light, four archangels who are my guides, and four directions. There was a lot at stake here and I felt a little anxious . . . okay, downright fearful, about whether I could reach Kara on the other side of the veil that separates us from those who have gone "home." I called my guides again, in case they weren't listening the first time, then opened the door to the "other side" and said a protection prayer. I recognized the familiar feeling of warmth, like benevolence, and something like a comforting connection to everything. I pictured the image in my imagination. The loving-goodness looked like a glowing web of light, made up of kindness, love and compassion. *Nothing can harm me,* I reminded myself. *My intention is to help in the best way I can, to be of service to Creator.*

I began, drawing a beautiful woman at a gala on my sketchpad. "Kara is showing me an image of herself, and she's looking like a movie star!" With my sixth sense, I clearly saw the figure of a stunning woman wearing a gown. *Was she showing me some images of herself when she was on Earth, or was I looking at a celebrity arriving at the Oscars on the red carpet?*

"Well, she is showing me herself as a glamorous movie star in a long black dress, impeccably coiffed, surrounded by admiring fans." I was relieved and grateful that, first of all, Kara had shown up, and second, that I was able to have a clear line of communication with her. The rest of the reading flowed easily. Actually, it was a piece of cake, considering the powerful emotions on both sides of the veil.

I am not in control of who does or does not appear from the other side. Sometimes ancestors from a few generations back whom the client has never met, materialize. There are times when someone distant, like an old college professor shows up, or sometimes someone close appears, such as a parent. Making contact is dependent on a few things it seems: in part, on my state of mind and health, and partly on my ability to interpret the images. Making contact also depends on the spirit's ability to lower its heavenly vibration and communicate with me. Some folks on the other side are more skilled at this than others. But I have given up trying to figure the mystery out . . . I just work here.

"Yes," said Gigi, "she was glamorous to her peers, and I guess I could say that she was the star of her own movie. She had the 'x factor', and people were drawn by her charisma."

"She certainly owned the stage and looked the part," I said. "But I see that she had the 'flaw of celebrity': she didn't have enough self-respect, and as a matter of fact, I'm getting the feeling she believed she was unworthy in some way. Her low self-esteem seems to have caused her problems. Am I right?" I hoped I had not been too blunt with Gigi. I had been working on being more diplomatic.

"All too true," responded Gigi, graciously.

The scene in my imagination changed. Now I saw a shopping mall interior. I heard the noise and felt the bustle of shoppers. I was drawn to a particular store on the second floor, but could not make out the name.

"She is showing me a storefront in a mall. I think she is saying it is important. Does this ring a bell?"

"Yes, yes. Kara worked at the Vancouver Mall in a shop on the second floor," Gigi said, leaning in. She was getting excited now.

"I see the store from the inside and there is a door in the back, on the far right. It's a little shop that feels like a dress shop; there are tchotchkes on the shelves. She's showing me an image of herself in the back room with another person or, maybe two." I felt dark energy around one of the people there. They were tainting Kara's light. I drew the floor plan in the corner of the rendering with a little room in the back. I thought there might be someone who would visit her there.

"They are being naughty," I offered euphemistically, "and Kara's telling me this is where and when her trouble first started. Does this make sense?" I inquired, not giving all the details. I had to weigh if the information would be helpful or too painful at this point, so I tried to approach the topic as gently as possible.

"In retrospect, the information makes sense. She worked at a shop there, but the door was on the left."

I closed my eyes, accessing the intuitive information about the interior of the shop. Again, I saw the door on the right.

"I still see the door on the right," I said, now a bit tentatively, doubting myself.

"No," said Gigi adamantly, "it's on the left."

Oh, darn it, I thought. I hate when this happens. I stared intently at the image in my mind. I tried to put the door on the left, but it moved to the right again in my vision. Again I pulled the door over to the left and it moved itself right back. *Hmmm, all right then, I'll just keep going. It's only a small detail*, I admonished myself, and I was well over eighty percent correct, a yardstick I self-imposed. Nonetheless, I felt a little disappointed.

I was pretty sure this was Gigi's daughter Kara, who had really survived death—well her soul had anyway, because, heck, I was talking to her. Gigi was excited at the possibility that her daughter's spirit was in the living room with us and I was thrilled to have achieved contact.

Kara *did* live, just not where Gigi could touch her.

Kara's passing was the greatest single loss of Gigi's life and her suffering was beyond words, like an ache in her bones—beyond time, universal, a sickening torment shared among all mothers who have lost children. An empty space.

Yet at the same time there was an overwhelming joy. Gigi had felt her daughter's presence before, but now she trusted this connection on a deeper level. Our conversation was not new information, but good confirmation for her mother: Kara had survived physical death.

A young girl's bedroom came into view, tiny and sweet, with diaphanous blue fabric moving gently from a breeze. I breathed deeply and centered myself again. A warm flow of energy washed over me and I allowed my consciousness to become part of the scene. The sweet, dry smell of summer filtered through, and I could see the sheen of blue fabric, glistening and undulating in front of a small window.

"Did Kara have a sheer blue fabric, light blue I think, in her room as a little girl?" We sat in silence for a few moments as Gigi reconnoitered.

There was a long pause, before Gigi said, "Yes, she did! And she loved that room that I decorated for her. I had forgotten," said Gigi with a far-away tone, as she seemed to remember the little girl who blossomed joy in her world.

A crossroad came into view in my mind, then a meadow. I had the feeling Kara had been in this place before. A stream of information was coming quickly. The flow grew from a gentle tributary, to a river, then a torrent. I saw an image of a small meadow encircled by pine trees and I was shown a target—a practice target, possibly. As I merged with Kara's thoughts, I could sense her thoughts and feelings.

The spirit of Kara communicated with me, saying, *This was just a play, a movie! I had things to learn when I was alive, but I got caught up in the drama. Everything seemed so real.*

The difficult circumstances she found herself in were over-whelming, all just too much. I could feel what she was feeling. I (she) felt trapped, like there was no way out of the mess. Stalemate. I (Kara) just could not see a way to escape from a bad situation. Nothing made sense.

The overwhelming feeling of confusion and desperation was so heavy that the experience was draining my energy. I separated my consciousness from hers and floated up above the scene. My body inadvertently sighed.

On that Mother's Day, Kara went to a remote area for pistol target practice with a friend and they had fired off a few rounds. Then she had put the gun to her head.

Tears welled up in my eyes. Sometimes when my heart is open, it is hard to separate from the emotion of the reading, which was the case that day. I hesitated.

"Well, Kara is here and her spirit lives. She is showing me the scene in the forest and explaining that she felt there was no way out." I opened my eyes to check on Gigi, who was shaken but composed. "She realizes her choice in taking this action affected many people. She was confused and didn't mean to hurt you or anyone. I get the impression she had other lifetimes in which she had taken her life. That information can't be verified, but the energy feels old."

NOTE: The concept of reincarnation of the soul, which is eternal, involves returning to physical form in the mortal human body many times. At these times, the soul enters the baby and remains for a lifetime, only to leave when the person dies. A person's or animal's soul has a feeling of ancient intelligence and is made of some kind of light, I guess you could say, but it is hard for me to define this eternal-intelligent-creative aspect in words.

FROM MY VANTAGE POINT as an intuitive, when people die, they lose only their bodies and some memory, but the real essence of who they are continues to live. From what I've "seen" and from what I have learned from the many people I have read over the years, souls return to Earth to family-type groups. Our relatives are often the same souls or actors we've incarnated with before, but they act the part of different characters in our personal movie. Each lifetime is a different production drawn from the same actors' guild or what I and others call a soul-family group or cluster of loved ones.

In succeeding lifetimes, you might be the daughter, or father, or possibly a neighbor. Earth life has many of the characteristics of a scripted play, yet the wild card is free will. We seemingly choose our lifetime with help from our guides or help from a spiritual non-physical being.

This idea that we have free will, and choose our life circumstances, sheds a completely different light on suffering. If we can choose, for example, to be born into a life with difficult circumstances, then it is impossible to claim victim status. So "I didn't ask to be born" is erroneous.

Although this is what I believe, I am not one-hundred percent sure of the scenario I am observing. But what this revolutionary idea guarantees is a shifting of the mindset from powerless to empowered; the cultivation of new directions; insight; and, ultimately, wisdom and happiness. By shifting awareness from the concept of being merely a movie character battered around by the winds of fate, or a cosmic screenwriter, a person becomes the main character of their own movie.

Free-will choices may seem small or huge, but they impact the soul profoundly, as, for example, leaving the "movie", or lifetime, early by taking one's own life. While it does not appear there are punishments on the other side of life and death for leaving by committing suicide, it does seem there are ramifications for the soul that has made that choice, or a karmic consequence of the action taken.

"Kara is showing me an image," I continued, "of herself holding a baby. She is in some kind of nursery on the other side. Looks like heaven's nursery. How cool," I commented. "There are cribs lined up, and she is telling me she spends time taking care of these babies. Her energy is strong. She is radiant, glowing with love. Gigi, she is happy. Most important of all, she is at peace."

Gigi looked ten years younger.

"Did she like babies in this life? Because it sure feels like she did."

"Kara worked at a daycare center. The children fell in love with her and she loved them right back. She was one of the most popular workers there and extremely talented with babies," Gigi said.

"I sense the babies I'm seeing her with now must have died for some reason and have returned home to heaven where she is helping them. I feel she is being guided to nurture them and that doing this work is important for healing, as well as to learn something. Maybe this is happening she won't make this choice again in the next lifetime. I'm not absolutely sure of this, but I gather that she is learning life on Earth is a priceless treasure, a gift given to us. Our bodies are only on loan. We don't own them, but they are a vehicle for an earthly journey," I said, half to myself.

"She is in a good place and it is fine that she is learning," I

HE WILL BE STRONG
LIKE A STALLION

continued. "She is also telling me she really appreciates her stepfather. They were not close, but she is deeply grateful for how well he treats you. She says he really adores you!"

Gigi smiled to herself. Leif, I later learned, was a devoted, loyal husband and her best friend. (I am glad to say I have come to count Leif as a dear friend also.)

As I rested again and found my center, galloping hooves thundered in my head. I got the impression of a shining black stallion on a hilly knoll, his mane flowing in the wind, his nostrils flared. He was proud and powerful: I realized the stallion represented Kara's son, Cole. Was Kara telling me, through symbols, that her son was strong and powerful? The horse was wild, but Cole was just an eleven-year-old boy. Maybe she was telling me about a potential future. She seemed to indicate the stallion should be "broken in," meaning he should not run wild.

I intuited that Kara appreciated her mother's structured approach with Cole, which I assumed included a homework policy, discipline, and a predictable home life. Kara was communicating beyond words that Cole would grow up to be a force for good in the world, and that if he stayed on the straight and narrow, he would turn out well—very well.

Kara had one more important message for Cole, and it was distinct. I could discern the warm and intimate communication effortlessly.

"Gigi, Kara wants Cole to know she loves him. That she will always be watching over him."

I took a deep breath to slow my racing heart. I felt a mother's endearment, adoration, and tiger-love for her child. I had hit a vein of gold, if not the motherlode of love, an emotion so powerful it can move mountains. Cole's loss seemed so heavy, the price too great. His life had changed profoundly on that Mother's Day.

"Sometimes he will be able to feel her presence, like when he is sitting at the computer at his desk." I went on to describe the desk's location in his bedroom. "Cole will feel his mother as a warm wave of love."

We were silent for a while. I got the impression of flying, and I could feel the sensation of soaring high, with warm air under my wings. A thermal? *Somehow it is significant*, I thought. *Maybe she will come back as a bird.* "I get a feeling from Kara that's something to do with a bird's flight . . . hmmm . . . was she a pilot? She may take the form of a bird. I know that might sound strange, but spirits have the capacity to influence the material world. I have seen that happen many times. Animals are a common way spirits communicate with those still alive on Earth. Anyway, I'm just putting this thought out there. I feel there may be an important visit from a fine-feathered friend, if you know what I mean."

"Wow, Kara would talk about flying in her dreams a lot. And that's more than interesting, because she told Cole she would be with the birds."

Gigi went on to explain that during the times Kara was in rehab or out on a binge, Cole would have a hard time because he missed his mother so much. Kara would comfort him by telling him she was with him always, that if not by his side, she would be in a flock of birds, so he should just look out the window.

"If Cole keeps his eyes open he will be able to recognize Kara. More importantly, he must keep his heart open. When the time is right, let him know he could not have stopped her suicide. That action was about her, *not* Cole. She chose 'door number two', if you will, and from what I get, she was terrified and confused about a lot of things. She loves him more than words can say. Going home to heaven early was her choice. Please let him know her death wasn't his fault. Her situation was beyond him and there was nothing he could have done to change the outcome. His love was enough for her — *he* was enough, but not enough to make her stay. No one was. She was just in too much pain."

I gave Gigi some emotional space and silence to digest all the information. The reading was getting to be a little tiring for me, too . . . actually, exhausting, if I'm truthful. Then my head started pulsing with energy and the epicenter seemed to be coming from something in the corner of Gigi's kitchen. I knew the energy signature was crystal; it also felt goddess-like, maybe like Shiva or Quan Yin.

"Is there a crystal in the corner of the window in your kitchen? She's showing me something in the corner that has energy, something that might make rainbows when the light hits it. It is important somehow," I said.

"That is where I have a crystal and a little statue of a guardian angel that I placed there for her. That's also where I talk to her," answered Gigi.

"She is sending me a feeling of gratitude," I responded. "She truly appreciates your prayers and good wishes. They are helping her where she is now. The rainbows are energetic manifestations from the other side of how your focused prayer looks to her. That energy is helping her heal." (This is another example of how we affect our loved ones on the other side.) "She is grateful for the home life and wonderful family environment you created for her. She does NOT want you to feel guilty. Her suicide was NOT your fault either," I cautioned.

A feeling of unconditional love enveloped me, like a stadium of 30,000 souls clapping and cheering. Kara was trying to make sure I didn't miss the cue and I could feel my energy field bloom and expand in response. Kara was sending a message to her mother: I love you, huge.

"She's showing me how much she adores you, big time. You were the best . . . I mean you are the best. Bravo and a standing ovation from a packed Olympic-sized auditorium!"

I must say I feel so fortunate that I am allowed to experience the energy that spirits send to loved ones. This experience has unequivocally changed the way I see the world. Through the gift of being able to communicate with spirits on the other side, I have a much better understanding that truly, love never dies. Love lives, persists, and survives. When Einstein said energy can't be destroyed, it can only be changed, I wonder if he was considering the possibility that the concept could apply to the soul or spirit?

"She is showing me an image of Cole. She's letting me know she appreciates everything you are doing for her son, your grandson, and that she loves Cole deeply and profoundly. Kara is helping you with him every day."

Gigi had felt all along that her daughter was alive somehow, someplace, in some form. The reading confirmed her suspicions and in a way showed the worst was over. Now the messages of eternal love from Kara could sink in, and of course while the pain of loss would never go away, at least the healing could start.

"So she's okay and well," said Gigi, with a dazed tone. "Is there anything I can do for her?"

I scribbled the place-setting on my sketchpad of the kitchen island I saw in my imagination and, sure enough, Kara was sitting in the chair in front of it, waiting.

"She would like you to set a place for her. I see a mat, napkin, plate—the works. She is showing me the counter in your kitchen by the wall. Kara would like you to put out a setting there and have lunch with her once in a while."

"Of course I will. I would be happy to," said Gigi.

"Now I see a large bird on your back deck or yard. It's big, but I'm not sure what I'm looking at. An eagle? No, maybe a hawk. Hmm, giant owl? No, I think it is a woodpecker. Anyway, this bird is BIG. This might be symbolic, because sometimes it's hard for me to tell if I am looking at a real event or a symbol that represents something." Symbolism is the communication mode most often used by spirits on the other side to help me communicate. "This is a message from your daughter. Does this mean something to you?"

"Yes," Gigi said, appearing stunned. "The day Kara took her life, Cole and I saw a gigantic blue heron. The great crane had a huge presence as it flew the length of our house and I could see a good bit of detail. I remember the feet hung down. The great blue heron's wing almost touched the eaves of the house and I have never seen that happen before or since. I've lived here all my life and they just don't come that close to civilization."

Gigi pointed her finger from east to west, marking the bird's flight path. The same path the Life Flight helicopter had taken.

Chills went down my spine. It certainly appeared Kara had sent a message loud and clear, one Gigi understood completely.

I RAN TO CATCH MY phone that was buried somewhere beneath all the coats on the front bench in my home.

I hadn't heard from Gigi for a while, so I was pleasantly surprised when I heard her voice. "Hi Jane. I just happened to be in the Vancouver Mall doing some Christmas shopping and I walked past the store where Kara used to work. You know, the one you saw in our reading? By the way, the door IS on the right side after all!"

AS I WATCHED INCENSE MEANDER toward the bright prayer flags during Kara's funeral at a Tibetan center, I made a deal with God. In a "deal with the Big Guy," I promised that as my spiritual service work, I'd walk with Gigi weekly for a year. We rarely missed our walks, rain or shine, sleet or frozen rain— and in the Pacific Northwest we have it all.

We walked at Round Lake, a beautiful forested park with myriad paths. A metal bridge spanning a river that is gentle in fall and a raging torrent in spring was our turn-around point.

I would guide Gigi onto the old steel bridge and we'd stand over the moving water. "I need to throw in all that I no longer need to carry," I would say, and with that, I would toss in my worries and troubles. Gigi would too.

After the year was up, I confided to Gigi the promise I'd made at the funeral. In retrospect, helping her through the worst year of her life was repaid tenfold, because during that year we grew from friends to sisters.

KARA REPEATEDLY GOT ME OUT of bed at 3:00 or 4:00 a.m. to write her story, or at least that is what I surmised. I would feel a tap on my forehead or hear a loud clap . . . sometimes I went back to sleep, only to be roused later. At the time, I was writing her story and had allowed myself to get mired in details, which developed into a severe case of writer's block. I would find myself in front of my computer in the early hours of the morning, staring blankly, yet with an urgency to complete her narrative. She was persuasive—make that stubborn—but this book would never have been written without her. Once I was finished with the first edits, Gigi and I went over what I'd written to be sure the details were correct. She was surprised I had named Kara, "Diana", using a different name for Kara at first, as I had changed the personal details for privacy before the family had gave permission to use real names. Diana was the name that had come to me. Gigi was surprised because Diana was the name of Gigi's infant sister who had died.

The loss of Diana impacted Gigi's youth greatly. Somehow she had known her sister's soul would find its way back as her daughter in this life. When she was pregnant a third time, the name "Diana" was seriously considered, but in the end they named their daughter Kara instead.

© JANE DE FOREST

A GREAT BLUE HERON STARTLED me in the forest while I was on my daily walk. Its huge wingspan made for an awkward landing in a tree. I could feel Kara's presence and looked up the symbolic meaning of heron on my phone while in the midst of this beautiful forest that's covered with layers of green moss.

A few days later, I shared my heron research and Kara's connection with Gigi while on a walk together in the same lovely park. The glorious day took us down my favorite path by the river to our bridge, to throw "what we no longer need to carry" over the edge and watch it float away. On the return trip, as we rounded the corner, there was a stack of eleven rocks about two feet tall, neatly and precariously piled in the middle of the swiftly moving stream. I took a picture and wondered out loud if this was a prayer.

The rocks hadn't been there ten minutes before on our way down. They felt like a message from Kara.

In an inconceivable turn of events, as we discussed the mysterious stacked rocks and the heron's awkward landing, another great blue heron flew overhead. Gigi and I looked at each other and smiled.

Distant thunder sounded, with a rumble that seemed to shudder through my soul. A bright red Life Flight helicopter flew overhead . . . from east to west.

THE GREAT BLUE HERON (ARDEA HERODIAS) IS A LARGE WADING BIRD IN THE HERON FAMILY. A BLUE HERON IS THE LARGEST NORTH AMERICAN HERON, COMMON NEAR WETLANDS OVER MOST OF NORTH AMERICA AND CENTRAL AMERICA. THE AVERAGE LIFESPAN IN THE WILD IS FOURTEEN YEARS AND THE BIRD HAS A WINGSPAN UP TO SIX-AND-A-HALF FEET.

About a year later, Gigi, her husband Leif, and my husband and I sat around our fire pit, watching the sunset. We were discussing Kara's story as a great blue heron gracefully flew above our heads from east to west. A little while later when we discussed the concept that the afterworld was a fairytale invented to comfort people, the serendipity turned to shock and awe. We watched, mouths gaping, as another (or the same?) heron moved across the pink sky of day's end, from west to east.

A LETTER FROM GIGI

JANE IS A GIFTED VISIONARY. A reading with Jane is a journey that allows us to remember and know that love is an unbreakable connection.

Jane's reading presented me with a message of love and connection with my daughter on the other side. I experienced it on all levels of my being and the communication revealed and validated to me the limitless power of love. Jane's reading built a golden bridge between the world of illusion and separation that we live in, and the world of perfect love. After Jane's reading, all the barriers were removed between me and my beloved daughter on the other side, and remain so. The illusion of separateness disappeared and I know she is with me always.

Gigi
PORTLAND, OREGON

"Death is a natural part of life.
Rejoice for those around you who transform into the force."
YODA, STAR WARS

CHAPTER 2

In Heaven They Also Speak Chinese

© TARA DE FOREST

In Heaven
They Also
Speak Chinese:
A Love Story
個愛情故事

In the following story, initials represent real names, while other names have been changed. The location and all other details are factual.

"Being deeply loved by someone gives you strength, while loving someone deeply gives you courage."

LAO TZU

HER NAME WAS LEE. As a teen, she emigrated with her family from China and eventually ended up at Harvard University doing medical research. She opened a Chinese herbal and acupuncture clinic in the rural outback of a small Pacific Northwest town. At that time, anything other than Western medicine was considered quackery. Nevertheless, her practice eventually blossomed and thrived, and Dr. Lee became recognized as a healer by both the American and Chinese communities.

When I first met Lee, there was instant chemistry, as if I had known her from somewhere before. I could feel our connection in my bones. There was clarity in the quality of light emanating from her eyes. She spoke of the Tao, the teachings of Buddha, and of the universal life-force energy that flows through all. Her dream was to open a school where children would learn these teachings and uncover the truth within themselves to make the world a better place. I, too, secretly harbor that dream.

YB (his initials) was Lee's husband and soul mate; he towered over six-feet. His kind eyes and humble manner touched my heart. YB's integrity was reflected in his devotion to his family, his code of ethics, and the high standards he held himself accountable to. He, too, also felt familiar, and soon my heart loved YB like a younger brother.

YB had moved to the United States from mainland China in his youth. A keenly intelligent, handsome and ambitious young man, he assimilated quickly to Western culture and became a successful engineer in the semiconductor industry. Twenty years before, YB and Lee had met at a mutual friend's wedding in New York. After spending a magical time at the reception, talking and, later on, Skyping, they had fallen deeply in love. The second time they met in person was sixty days later at their wedding altar. By all accounts, Lee was stunning as a bride in a white satin, beaded wedding gown, and YB looked the part of the handsome groom in a tuxedo with jasmine in his lapel.

Lee encouraged YB to call me for an intuitive business consultation (little did either of us know, his mother had other plans for the reading). I was prepared with my drawing paper and pencil, having cleared the space with holy water and prayers in preparation for the meeting. When YB arrived, he looked a bit harried—his life seemed to have him running pretty hard.

As I closed my eyes and centered myself, his light, the essence of who he is, started to come into focus. Whatever this light is, I know its essence is divine, and perhaps represents the soul or spirit. In YB's energy field, his light was bright, wise and wide, all telltale signs of an old soul, or at least that is what I've deduced from my intuitive readings over the years. The divine energy has many names: flow of Tao, grace, chi, prana—and is what feeds us energetically. I see it as the light of a person and often that light takes the shape of their ideology, acculturation and life experience. The light takes the form of how and what we think, and is the filter through which we see reality.

In YB's light I detected a blockage in the flow of his energy field. I sketched the silhouette of his figure, a shadowy area with a dark center and a bright expansive area over his head. Although he appeared free from most of the negative patterns that plague many of the people I see, his energy nevertheless drooped down at the edges like a large Casa Blanca lily starved for water. Typically, this is an indicator that a client's vitality, physical health and strength are weak. My experience told me he was exhausted and that reconnecting to nature would help him immeasurably.

The quandary? How best to convey the information. My goal is to get through to the person in their own language or code. Everyone has their own personal intuitive code, or internal symbolic language, based on personal history, perception and style. Formulating the message is akin to speaking a foreign language—with me as translator. Just as speaking Bulgarian to a Samoan (unless, by chance, they know Bulgarian) won't get me far, I try to serve up the relevant information in a way that makes sense. Determined to find the most effective approach, I decided on a direct delivery.

"YB, you are exhausted," I began.

His eyebrows rose as he slumped back in his chair. He seemed grateful that I could recognize his current predicament.

Score, Jane, I told myself.

"Jane, I work a demanding job as an engineer in the high-tech industry—my two-hour commute is hard and often I help my family by cooking meals, taking the kids to their lessons . . . oh, and I help with their homework too. I do whatever I can for my elderly father, JZ," he said proudly, "and yes, I am completely exhausted."

"I see you're totally wrung out," I said, acknowledging him. "But I also see your positive attitude and right actions reflected in the quality of your light. The essence of who you are is truly magnificent. I see you have a lot of personal power. This is a good sign," I emphasized, reflecting his exquisite nature back to him. "Let me hold space for you in compassion."

I took a moment.

"You're definitely in a tough spot on account of your physical and mental fatigue. Please, make yourself comfortable in your chair, close your eyes and follow your breath. I am going to do a short meditation with you."

As I sat across from YB at my large antique desk, I also closed my eyes in meditation. Centering, I breathed deeply as my energy field opened. Observing YB's difficult situation, my heart swelled in empathy, allowing me to feel compassion. I held his suffering spaciously within my open heart, without judging or trying to fix his pain. I imagined my compassionate energy as shimmering peacock blue, and enveloped him within that energy. Then I imagined a golden white blanket of energy, imbued with love, surrounding YB.

After a few minutes, the presence of a female spirit became palpable. She felt strong, determined. I communicated "welcome," telepathically acknowledging her. I held my hand up, indicating for her to please wait for a moment, as I had more to tell YB. The female spirit moved back a bit, but did not go far. Her power, love and purposeful intent hung thick in the air.

The details of YB's energy signature gradually revealed itself on the drawing paper, as I sketched with my 6B pencil. I shadowed a thirsty, energy lily-flower emanating from his interior, reaching far past the image of his physical body. A line across the bottom of his figure indicated where his chi energy was cut off. If I could only help him understand how his thoughts were affecting his field, I knew he would feel more rejuvenated and less tired. A feeling of strength and power arose within my energy field. In my imagination I saw YB at his highest poten-

© TARA DE FOREST

tial. The symbolic lily was strong and his vital chi was back
... I could feel him. I realized I was experiencing his pure and
most self-realized state, and I felt a jolt.

"YB, you are disconnected from . . . well . . . hmm, from, ya
know . . . God," I blurted.

I wasn't sure exactly how to present the idea of the Divine,
but it was obvious the concept of "God" missed the mark. He
looked at me quizzically. Since YB didn't see God as a person-
ification of the Divine, the concept didn't fit. I watched with
my eyes closed as the form of his belief-structure took shape
above his head.

My pencil flew. I sketched and shaded.

I drew a swirling energy flow that connected him to a network
circling the globe. I had a feeling of Taoism as I drew, then
Confucianism, then a broad grasp of the meaning of Divine
light. I drew the link to his ancestors that I saw—and it felt
like Animism. This was new for me; I was not sure what I was
looking at.

Hmm, a little tricky to draw, Jane.

IN THE TAOIST TRADITION, THERE really isn't God, as such,
but rather, "the way", which includes a recognition of the flow
of energy through all things, an underlying principle of the
balance of opposites (yin and yang), and harmony with nature.
Confucianism is inherent in Asian philosophy, which emphasizes harmonious social structure and honorable and ethical
behavior in society.

Consequently, the influence of Animism in the Asian culture (also ubiquitous in all indigenous cultures) is characterized by a reverence for nature and for the ancestors. Ancestors are an integral part of everyday life; the veil between the world of the living and the world of the dead is practically nonexistent. There is a deep understanding that life and death are part of the same cycle. But most important is the notion that everything in nature is alive, eternal, and everyone and everything are all inside this web of existence.

We humans tend to want to specifically brand the light as either a religion, as God (or gods), or as nature. When I read a client intuitively, the divine light takes on the shape of a person's mental structure, which is in part a byproduct of their particular beliefs and of how they think. I try my best to put the light that I see into terms people can relate to. After twenty years of practicing Vipassana meditation (okay, not every day), and studying Eastern religions, I have a general idea of the Eastern concept of the Divine—and so I decided to couch my thoughts in Asian terms.

"YB, I feel your 'monkey mind' is too busy to allow awareness, er, your chi is depleted, hmm, you are not in the primary flow of the Tao," I stumbled. I began again. "Nature feeds you, and that is where your pranic life-force energy becomes strong and where you are at your most healthy and happy. You can best connect with what's real when you're in nature, and with what's authentic inside you when you become still."

He must have recognized his dilemma, because there was awareness behind his eyes. I had spoken to his heart, although which concept had struck a chord, I couldn't be sure. Delivering an accurate cross-cultural message had meant relying on my limited knowledge of Eastern philosophies and religions. My assignment was to translate symbolic intuitive information first into English, then into Chinese concepts, so YB could accept and use the message in his life. In fact, YB's belief system was "unbranded", all-inclusive, and incorporated the truth that resides in all religions.

"Grounding to the earth will help your fatigue," I said, as I saw a light coming from the soles of his feet, going down into the earth and back again. "There is something popular now called 'grounding'—essentially, just old-fashioned walking on the earth with bare feet. Doing this will help you heal and replenish the life-force energy that connects you to the flow of life. Please consider lying on the ground every day. Bend your knees and make sure the soles of your feet touch the earth."

My drawing pencil started to fly as I sketched a picture of YB. I rendered the shape of his chi energy and illustrated his life from the vantage point of my intuitive awareness. However, peering at his "field" with my eyes closed, I saw a strange greenish light with an odd vibration—I saw this was irritating his body.

"I see your workspace has a strange light. Might this also be a sound frequency? The room seems to have a greenish hue and I feel uncomfortable when I look at the scene from here in my consciousness."

"I am in the semiconductor industry," he responded. "In the area where we make the chips, there is microwave technology. And yes, in making semiconductors there is a greenish light and frequency from the production area. You're right."

"Your body is telling me the light and the frequency are agitating you. Contact with a natural environment will soothe your discomfort and calm your energy field."

Just as I was about to describe the scene to YB, I felt an impact on my chest, like a hard punch. I was stunned and caught off guard. The wind had been knocked out of me!

Yet at the same time I felt an overwhelming wave of motherly love: warm, nurturing, safe and all accepting. Tears welled up in my eyes and tingles went down my spine. The female spirit who had appeared from the other side earlier now became more prominent. Was this spirit capable of affecting me like that?

Had she love-whacked me?

Had she reached through the veil between the worlds and given me an energetic left hook?

YB peered at me. I was confused, unsure of what was happening. I wished I could explain the strange scene to him, but I had no idea what was going on.

"YB, there's a spirit present and I think she may be an ancestor, perhaps your mother or grandmother. She has a strong female energy and is, well, determined," I said, gasping for breath as I reached for the tissue box to blot my tears.

"Oh, that would be my mother," he stated factually, in his heavy Mandarin accent. "She was tough cookie."

"Well, I would say she *still* is a tough cookie." I smiled, admiring a son's respectful recognition of his mother's strength.

This was an excellent opportunity to communicate with YB's mother, but I wanted to make sure the spirit really was his mother. My standard protocol to establish the true identity of a spirit from the other side is to ask for specific information of which I'd have no way of knowing beforehand.

I invited her to communicate more clearly with my mind, and the image of the translucent woman came more opaque. Sketching the outline of her figure, I blocked in her black hair, swept up with golden hair ornaments. Her red and blue jacket was prominent; she was trying to indicate its importance. My textile background served me well, as I intuited silk batting between two pieces of heavy silk brocade, covered in shiny embroidery. I described the costume I saw to YB in detail.

His eyes penetrated mine with "the look." I am not completely unfamiliar with "the look", which typically indicates something I have just said has hit home—that I've nailed something so personal, so private, that no other human being knows the secret. YB took a moment to compose himself.

What I had told him, in fact, was an accurate description of the 17th-century Qing Dynasty jacket preserved in a garment bag in his father's home. The jacket was his mother's most precious possession, given to her great-great grandmother by the Chinese empress in appreciation for her husband's service as physician to the Imperial family and court.

"Jane, that is remarkable! The jacket is red and blue padded silk with silk embroidery," he confirmed.

I felt satisfied this was an authentic communication with his mother, so I allowed myself to proceed. She sent me another image: two people in armchairs, silhouetted against a picture window. I knew somehow that the figures were his mother and father, together. I had a strong feeling this was a significant message. But the heart-to-heart communication was not intended for YB at all. The message came across as "urgent." And it was meant instead for his father, JZ.

A PROFESSOR OF MICROBIOLOGY AND horticulture at the prestigious Fudan University in Shanghai, YB's father, JZ, had been a respected intellectual. He had been sent away to the countryside for "re-education" during China's Cultural Revolution. Approaching his mid-80s, the gaunt and fit Chinese man had smooth, tan skin stretched over high cheekbones, and sparkling, benevolent eyes. He was one of the most beautiful old men I had ever met. JZ had an air of peaceful wisdom, like an ancient sea turtle, and his kind heart and gentle awareness made me think he was the type that only comes to Earth once every 1,000 years. The elderly father and his wife had been married for forty-six years when she passed away the year before this reading with their son. Although his sweet grandchildren filled JZ's world, he continued to feel an aching loneliness. He missed his wife terribly. She was the greatest love of his life.

Well-dressed in her exquisite embroidered vestment, her spirit now motioned to her right. My right arm pulsed. I knew in the core of my being this was an important gesture.

"YB, your mother is showing me an image of two people in chairs by a large window. She is insisting that something important is on the right. I don't know what is important here, but I feel a lot of emotion."

"Yes, they sat together in front of the big picture window overlooking their backyard and watched the birds and squirrels at the feeder. Her chair was the one on the right. She always sat on my father's right side. It's the old Chinese way originating from the Taoist philosophy of Yin and Yang, Women are Yin, always on the right, the husband, a man, is Yang and on the left," clarified YB.

The rest of his mother's message for her husband would come later, but I refocused on YB.

"YB, your mother is telling me you are remorseful about something. Whatever you are worrying about, she does not want you to feel bad," I said, observing the shadow in his energy field.

During his mother's final year, the family had swooped in to help and nursed her until the end. A devoted son, YB had been hit hard by his mother's death. He now revealed that although he had tried to be a good son, he nevertheless was convinced he'd failed his mother. He told how he'd stayed with his mother on her last evening, but that around midnight, he'd headed home because he had work and the kids had school the next day. She died at 2:00 that morning.

Her son had missed her final breath by two hours. Tragically, he felt great remorse that his mother had died and he hadn't been there for her.

How could he ever forgive himself?

"Look YB," I told him, "your mother is showing me that she is always with you. She loves you tons. That you missed her departure doesn't seem to matter to her at all. What's important to her is that you not carry the burden of shame or guilt. The weight is too heavy and a waste of your vital chi energy. She wants you to be free of these negative feelings and she seems completely without anger or blame. She wants you to let the burden go and she is showing me only that she is grateful and appreciates all that you did for her."

His mother was beaming. She seemed happy I had gotten the message straight. A wave of pride came over me as I saw her looking up at him and saw the image of a pedestal—she thought the world of him. There was no doubt that she loved and respected her son, an easy symbol to decipher.

"YB, your mother is communicating from the other side that she is overjoyed with you. She respects and loves you more than life itself, and that is the truth. Please consider changing your perception and your thoughts about what happened."

"I am not sure what you mean, Jane." He looked perplexed.

"The feelings of remorse, disappointment and regret have an energy field, and I can see the effect when I look at your *chi* life-force. Focused negative energy can create a block in the flow of *chi*. Think of universal life-force energy or *chi* as a river that is continually flowing; then imagine large rocks, even a huge boulder, in the way. Just as the rock is an obstruction to the flow of water in the river, your remorse is blocking your vital chi flow.

"When people change their perception or thoughts about an incident from negative to positive, their blocks shift or even dissipate. The process is absolutely fascinating and allows for greater vitality and happiness. In other words, think differently and your reality will change in real time."

"That's all fine and good, Jane, but how am I supposed to change my perception about something that already happened? A real fact is a real fact! I let her down, that is the truth, I can't lie to myself. It would be dishonorable to make up a different story," he stated firmly.

The notion that to change your perception about a real, historical event can change the reality of that event, its dynamics or meaning may seem fantastical.

Magical thinking?

Yes.

It takes an open mind to entertain the idea that the effect of what happens to you is often more about the story you tell yourself than about the actual event. But putting the concept into practice works for many people and I have seen the miraculous results. My first step is to convince a person's logical mind to entertain the possibility that an event or idea might be three-dimensional, like a sphere, rather than flat. The truth is more than "right" or "wrong"—it is like a sphere, where both hemispheres are required to maintain each half. There is not a north without a south or east without a west.

If your mind can think outside its comfortable box and entertain the possibility of this paradox being true, for even a moment, a crack will begin to form in your mind's calcified and limited version of the truth. In the cracking comes uncertainty, but at the same time emerges the light of creativity, inspiration and growth that illuminates something authentic. In an instant, healing and emotional blocks can be seen to dissipate. I often see this during an intuitive consultation in the form of dark clouds or a hard shell, depending on the intensity of the negative energy and the duration of the thought or idea. Once a person's internal space is cleared of toxic thoughts, a vacuum draws, or allows, life-force energy or chi into the body. The more that person can continue to open and "look on the bright side", the more rapidly the blocks melt, like ice cubes in the August sun.

I was determined to get through to YB. I just had to phrase the concept so his mind would not reject the idea.

"YB, can you entertain the possibility that your mother wanted to die in the way she did? Maybe she waited until the exact right moment to go 'back Home', to avoid your suffering by witnessing her last breath? What if everything worked out the best possible way? What if the situation was actually perfect in its seeming imperfection?"

I was starting to sound like the shaman in Avatar.

YB had a distant look on his face. He had been carrying this weight in his heart since his mother's death. No one else knew his secret agony. Now the cat was out of the bag. I had seen through his exterior into the real him, his authentic self.

Sometimes that is all that is required to heal on a deep level, and will instantaneously eradicate decades of misery. This was colossal.

I lowered my head in prayer, giving them their privacy. I had more to tell him but sensed I should be quiet. I focused my attention on my breath, the rising and falling of my chest. Then with unconditional love, I imagined light glowing from my heart and bathing him, holding him in compassion.

"Yes, Jane, I think maybe I can give up the idea. If she wants me to let go, I will," he said, with a respectful nod I knew was meant for his mother, not me. YB, the obedient son that he was, would try his best to follow her instructions.

Smiling, I watched with my eyes closed, as his energy moved straight up and became filled, bigger. The block seemed to dissipate. *Chi* filled him and his energy was much brighter. His mother was glowing brightly. She seemed pleased with me, too—at least I hoped she was, after that energy slam to my heart.

"I think you just did let the block go, YB."

"You're right. I did change my perception of what I thought happened and maybe there are many ways to look at something. Yes, perhaps truth is not flat, but a spherical shape, where the vantage point of the observer defines as true the part of the truth that is visible. That way more than one 'truth' could coexist and still be right," he said, revealing his understanding.

I could sense his mother had more to tell him. YB was looking a little less nervous and a little more shell-shocked.

In many Asian cultures, a home shrine devoted to ancestors is prominent and daily offerings of food, water and incense are made with reverence. There is no taboo in the East about communicating with family members on the other side, like there is in the West. So the fact that his mother had come to visit him was the highest honor for a good son in Chinese culture, and he was proud.

We both smiled at each other. Again, I had a palpable feeling of pride wash over me. His mother wanted to make sure I wrapped up our conversation her way.

YB was right—she was a tough cookie.

A forceful pulse of electro-magnetic energy washed through my body, causing the back of my neck to tingle, then spread up my scalp. With my sixth sense, I saw the image of the same two chairs silhouetted against the picture window and a man and woman reappeared. The message was hard to miss.

"YB, your mother is finishing up, and I am getting a bit tired, as our reading has lasted almost two hours. But she wants to tell you two things. First, she unequivocally wants you to know she is very, very proud of you. You were an A+ son, and she has nothing but love and appreciation for you. The second thing she wants to convey is to please tell your father she still sits with him in her old chair by the window. She wants him to know he will see her again when the time is right." I felt my right arm tingle. "She is indicating, of course, that she is on his right, as usual."

AFTER STORY

I AM DEEPLY GRATEFUL TO this family for allowing me to tell their story. Communicating with a spirit on the other side who is from a completely different culture from my own was both challenging and transformative. The language of the spirit, or soul, seems to be universal, and this story underscored that fact for me. I speak three words of Chinese (quite well, if I do say so myself), and YB's mother spoke rudimentary English while on Earth. My knowledge of Chinese history, culture and art is only basic, but to my amazement, this cross-cultural and inter-dimensional communication was seamless—well, relatively seamless. Ultimately though, the love shared between this mother and her son transcended not only language and culture, but also time and space. There is a recurring theme that has revealed itself in my clients' sessions: once shared, love is never lost or destroyed. Love never dies.

© JANE DE FOREST

YB'S TESTIMONY

AN ORDINARY WEEKEND AFTERNOON transformed itself into one of the most deeply personal and memorable days of my life. It was the day I had an intuitive consultation with Jane de Forest. I have met many different kinds of people from all over the world, but somehow the powerful connection I experienced with Jane was instantaneous and unique.

Honestly speaking, I wasn't expecting too much from our session, BUT Jane proved me wrong. As an engineer, I can be logical and analytical; there is no column in my data-driven brain to input this type of nonscientific, nonlinear information.

But I was immersed in a wonderful moment of spiritual journey that Jane took me on that led me to be reconnected with my departed loved one, my beloved mother. The experience gave me a sense of inner peace and a calm feeling rushed into my soul. It was exactly what I needed in order to find that quiet place inside my mind/body and fill the gaping void in my heart. This was the first time in my life that I have ever been able to achieve this level of awakening. It was a lifting, which is difficult to put into words.

The entire session helped to lower the "rpm" of my busy and "high-rev" mind, and allowed me to experience something I never had before. Jane gently encouraged growth within me by pointing me to my own inner truth without any forceful language or actions. She gave me a sense of peace and connection and taught me some mindfulness techniques in order to let go of the stress and burden in my life. In addition, she has many years of knowledge and wisdom, and expresses passion for her work with integrity and love. Jane's reading carried a unique approach of spiritual connection to the universe, and she has an ability to help inquirers who are searching to find their way back to their path. My experience with Jane has been a forward step toward my inner peace and to helping me remember why I am here.

YB
VANCOUVER, WASHINGTON

© TARA DE FOREST

I believe that if I should die,
and you were to walk over my grave,
from the very depths of the earth
I would hear your footsteps.

BENITO PEREZ GALDOS

CHAPTER 3

I
LOVE YOU
TO THE MOON
AND BACK

© TARA DE FOREST

I Love You
To The Moon
And Back

*I am deeply grateful to Jerry for allowing me to tell his
story. All names, locations and details are factual.*

Where there is love, there is life.
MAHATMA GANDHI

L OVE NEVER DIES. Although mourning is an important
human custom and ritual, the love we have shared is
never lost, and no love is ever wasted. Love is a precious
jewel we can take with us when we leave this place. At least
that is what I have come to understand from the years I have
been a humble student of life after death.

My friend Jerry and I were relaxing during a rare windless
evening at Cannon Beach on the Oregon Coast. Robin, Jerry's
recently departed wife, had loved Canon Beach. Seabirds were
nesting on Haystack Rock, which towers 200 feet in the air,
and glorious tide pools were filled with bright purple starfish
nestled beside orange ones. We had visited them earlier;
the soft green sea anemones grabbed our fingers, thinking
they were tasty fish. A bright red crab was trapped in a deep
pool, having missed the outgoing tide, and seagulls watched
hopefully from overhead. We saw tufted puffins diving and
swimming to catch little fish and they seemed to cheer Jerry

up a bit. Their stocky little black bodies, white heads with black caps, bright orange feet and bills, made them look like adorable pets. Sandpipers with tweezer-like bills ran upon the sand, following the waves back and forth.

In this picturesque small-town village by the sea, we had seen the Shakespearean favorite, *Twelfth Night*, at Coastal Theater Playhouse. Afterwards, we built a fire on the beach. The driftwood crackled, the flames licked upward, and glowing sparks shot toward the dusk sky, captivating us. Sheer sandstone cliffs gave way to a vast expanse of beach where rocks the size of buildings dotted the rugged coastline. The sand was cool under our feet as we sat around a driftwood fire. In the darkening night sky the bright full moon rose, casting bluish-purple shadows across the scalloped sand; the silver reflections dancing on the rhythmic sea mesmerized us all. The joy of old dear friendships and unconditional love filled our hearts. Transfixed by the flames that warmed our faces,

the fresh, cool air at our backs, and the ocean's muted roar in the distance, we were possessed by a Buddha-like calm.

We laughed, talked, and remembered dear Robin. This night was the one-year anniversary of Jerry's wife's passing. One year ago that very night, she had died. Well, of course she really wasn't "dead" dead—she had left her cancer-ridden earthly garment behind, and the true essence of Robin had returned home.

In the peace of the star-filled night, we held reverent silence for Robin. We all took turns saying prayers and sending her our love and good wishes on the other side. The past year had been grueling for Jerry, the most difficult of his life.

"Look!" Jerry said suddenly, pointing behind our heads at the moon, startling us half out of our minds.

I saw something like a candle in a paper bag floating gently toward the star-filled sky. *Hmm, what is that . . . am I dreaming?* Hauntingly beautiful, magnificent little hot-air balloons floated weightlessly, snaking upward, like an E.E. Cummings poem. A dozen warm, luminescent flickering flames, juxtaposed against the cool dark cobalt sky.

"Chinese lanterns!"

The evening seemed like a dream; we watched spellbound as a group farther down the beach released the Chinese lanterns. I'm not sure how long we were there, but the men stayed a little longer as I returned to the cabin with my elderly mother.

Jerry explained later that for some reason he had felt an inexplicable urge to turn and watch the first lantern. The flickering renegade lantern rose far beyond the illuminated parade, possibly 1,000 feet, then pulled away from its group and headed straight for a low-hanging cloud. Though Jerry expected the cloud's moisture to extinguish the flame, he still kept searching for the solo flier.

Out the lantern popped, having penetrated the cloud.

Intrigued with the unfolding journey of the rogue Chinese lantern, he kept vigil, watching until the lantern became a black dot silhouetted against the full moon. Then, slowly, the shadow descended, falling back down to earth, swallowed by the evening's exquisite stillness.

© JANE DE FOREST

I HAD PROMISED JERRY AN intuitive reading, and was looking forward to the opportunity to help him. So the next morning we headed down to the beach before the family woke up. The summer day was a typical one for the Oregon Coast:

cold, wet and windy. I was wrapped in my Columbia fleece, wool hat, flip-flops, and a raincoat.

Jerry and I made a wind block with my half-dome tent and got comfortable. I breathed, centered, and prayed. My intuitive process of opening my sixth sense took a moment, but before long I felt the familiar, comfortable and warm feeling of connection, and impressions started coming fast.

I sensed her presence and felt like crying. "Robin is here now, and I love her," I said, remembering her lovely energy. We had met once before. "I see her and, my heavens, she is exquisite!" She was glowing with such magnificence—luminous strands floated in my mind and I could feel the tone of her life-force energy.

"She is wearing a long glimmering gown, and frankly the outfit's amazing. The dress is alive." Somehow intelligence seemed to be woven in. "I feel angelic energy and, well, hmm, the garment seems to have unconditional love inside. The trailing energy field looks like translucent gossamer film over her pulsating, glowing gown. The dress has flowing radiant streamers that feel like silent satin. I see floating diamonds, maybe crystals that refract the light, that are flashing a million tiny rainbows . . . my heavens, it's remarkable! I am amazed." I felt unable to do justice to the image. Words seemed inadequate and I was muddling up the vision.

"A psychic saw her in a long flowing dress, too, similar to your description," Jerry said.

"She is trying to give you a message . . . let me allow space in my mind to receive the communication clearly," I said.

"She was sharing the evening with us last night on the beach with the fire. I sure felt her, did you?" I was getting an awareness of the previous night and the moon, with a feeling about falling back to Mother Earth. "She is communicating something about the lanterns you saw."

In my imagination she expressed the idea she had joined us the night before. Because I had turned in early, I missed the rogue lantern's adventure, so I mistakenly thought she was telling me only that.

"She keeps showing me the moon, hmm, and the lanterns. Did the two of you share a significant memory that included Chinese lanterns?"

"No." Jerry wanted to make my story fit; he has a generous heart, which is one of the reasons I adore him.

I was hearing, seeing and feeling the message, but translating between the two worlds can be tricky sometimes. The language of the spirit world presents itself in symbols that need to be decoded, not unlike a dream. I could feel Robin's presence and her willingness to communicate with me, but I was missing the message. I decided to stop forcing the process.

Jane! I was losing my edge. Time for an adjustment. *Observe, Jane!*

I breathed in and followed my breath. Breathing out, I again followed my breath. I focused on the rising and falling of my chest as my breath entered me, animating me and releasing me. I observed the rising and falling of my chest, then I named my breath: "rising breath, falling breath." Then, I was back.

"Falling to earth—did you have a favorite song, one that belonged to just the two of you, such as *Walking On The Moon?*" I got creative.

"No."

Well, hmm, this is starting to be about as much fun as a root canal. I could feel Robin strongly. Sometimes things do not jibe until later, but I wished I could nail the reading right then.

"Did you have an inside joke, like 'she takes you to the moon?'" I queried.

"No, sorry Jane," he said kindly, but I'm sure he felt sorry for me by this time. I understood . . . I felt sorry for me too.

Fear approached and slithered into my belly. Anxiety felt like electricity spreading throughout my body. I prayed for help. *I can do this,* I told myself. *Piece of cake. Easy. I have helped people over the years, this is no different . . . pull yourself together, Jane. You have help.* I prayed hard to the "Big Guy."

"Let's try this one more time. Take you to the moon, bring you back, love you as big as the moon?" I said, grasping at straws, determined to overcome my adversity.

There was a long silence. The cool coastal wind whipped around our little tent and sand hit like tiny bullets. A seagull swooped down looking for a morsel, but there was only Jerry and me sitting cross-legged on my Pendleton woolen blanket with black, red, yellow and green stripes.

"I love you to the moon and back," said Jerry, putting the pieces together. "Robin said that to me every single day, and to the boys. Nobody knew. Just our family."

Phew, I got the message! Geez. My body let out an involuntary sigh. I could feel the tension drain from my face.

The Chinese lantern had gone "to the moon and back", a symbol of their undying and eternal love, in addition to a literal interpretation of the phrase that Robin repeated daily. That was the sign she was trying to send Jerry through me. She had most likely taken control of the first lantern, sending it far above the others. At least from my experience, some spirits seem to be able to influence matter.

"Of course Robin knows your mind and she knew we were getting together. So this may well be her opportunity to let you know she still 'loves you to the moon and back.' The love you share will never die and you will be reunited when the time comes."

His body shook gently and the soft sound of his weeping caught my ear. Compassion for his suffering welled up in that tender moment.

He let out a moan. His pain was primordial, a sound from a deep, ancient place in his soul now separated from the partner with whom he'd shared thirty years of love, family, bills, cele-brations, worries, illness, graduations, failures and triumphant births. Robin was the mother of his children, his soulmate, best friend and his lady.

Soon Jerry's body was shaking violently. I kneeled next to him and put my hand on his chest and back. I felt his broken heart between my hands. My heart held space for his pain. If pressed, I could not accurately measure the time. I "saw" layer after layer of past lives they had shared, fading back into the mists of time and stretching into the potential future. Their experience together was ancient and had had millennia to develop. Throughout time they had lived together in many cultures during various periods, switching genders, economic status and race. Their love continued into the future, too.

Jerry's sobbing turned to a quiet, peaceful calm. The rhythmic waves of the ocean surrounded us, and the moment seemed timeless.

"Well, brother, I think she really is here and she 'loves you to the moon and back.'"

We sat for a while, on the striped Pendleton blanket at the windblown coast, and then wandered back to the beach cabin. Most everyone was up, and I could smell bacon and onions frying. Life is good: love, friendship, and this eternal moment.

© TARA de FOREST

UNTIL WE MEET AGAIN

A LETTER FROM JERRY

EVEN THOUGH I'VE BEEN in the spiritual/New Age business since 1997 (I have a bookstore), I was still a bit skeptical about these sorts of "professed abilities." I've known Jane since 1996, and aside from knowing she was an awesome artist, wife and mother, for a long time I had no idea she had this ability.

Jane offered to do a reading for me shortly after my wife Robin passed. I didn't really know what she meant by a "reading," but I knew whatever she had in store would be beneficial. When she told me she was going to try to connect with Robin, I was shocked, excited, and some-what skeptical. I couldn't help but wonder if what I was about to hear was simply Jane's memory of Robin.

During that first reading, Jane was describing things that in some ways were spot on, and in other ways were not. So at Jane's insistence, I asked a question she would have no knowledge of, one that was vague enough to appease my skeptic side with an un-guessable answer. The question I posed was: "What was different about my sleep patterns last night?"

What Jane reported had me reeling. She said, "Robin says that what was different with your sleep patterns was 'the fact that you finally slept in our bedroom last night!' And that you slept on Robin's side of the bed!" Bingo, this was exactly what I was looking for. For a couple of weeks after she passed, I couldn't sleep in our bedroom, and I couldn't sleep on that old bed of ours either! I had been sleeping in a spare bedroom and had finally ordered a new mattress, which was delivered the day before this reading.

Robin was able to communicate to Jane a fact that indicated, beyond a shadow of a doubt, something that nobody else could have known. I knew then for myself that the process with Jane was real.

Fast forward to the one-year anniversary and the 'I Love You to The Moon and Back' story. I'd been blessed to have Jane do a number of readings for me prior to the one on the beach. For whatever reason, I was nervous about this session, as I reflect back now, maybe because I knew the emotional piece would be powerful.

The overpowering urge I'd experienced to turn around and look for that one lantern which was seemingly lost in the clouds—that was real! It happened, just as if I was tapped on the shoulder and directed upward. When I'd connected the dots, and the message of the Chinese lantern was clear, I just broke down. Robin was communicating that she still "loved me to the moon and back"— how could any message from my wife in heaven be any more powerful than that? I was happy, and knew that my angel of thirty years had transformed into an angel who now watched over me.

This experience taught me, even more than that Jane has an amazing gift that can help many people, to pay attention to what is unfolding around me. Watch for the signs, the things that in some way help you to remember a person who has passed on. The signs are there, if only you pay attention.

Jerry Miner
Gallatin, Tennessee

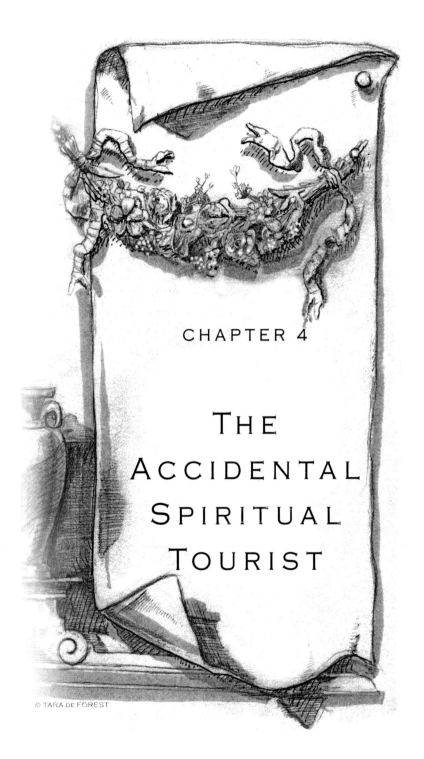

CHAPTER 4

THE
ACCIDENTAL
SPIRITUAL
TOURIST

© TARA DE FOREST

THE ACCIDENTAL
SPIRITUAL TOURIST

ALL ABOUT ME

*I've been absolutely terrified every moment of my life–
and I've never let it keep me from doing
a single thing I wanted to do.*

GEORGIA O'KEEFFE

EGYPT

M Y FASCINATION WITH THE ANCIENT world took me to Egypt. In the king's chamber of the Great Pyramid, while lying in the stone box surrounded by thirty-three fellow seekers chanting a peace prayer, I had a vision of the universe and simultaneously a profound understanding. The vision I saw in great detail impacted my understanding of this creation—I believe it opened up my sixth sense in a way that allowed me to perceive more clearly.

Aptly named *Initiate's Journey Through the Mystery School of Ancient Egypt*, the tour was led by two of my favorite teachers: prolific author Gregg Braden, and the native Egyptian and scholarly Egyptologist, Hakim. The group was slated to visit the ancient temple sites that had served as educational and training centers for the high priesthood of ancient Egypt.

Initiation into the highest realm of the ancient, established priesthood was obtained through education and rigorous tests in their mystery school system. This would be akin to a PhD in theology required for a leader in a religious career today, or equivalent to advanced seminary training, for a bishop or cardinal, but with accompanying physical and psychological ordeals . . . like swimming with crocodiles.

© TARA de FOREST

We secured private entry to the archeological sites before they opened to the public, and having the Great Pyramid to ourselves after it had closed was beyond remarkable. Our coach drove all day straight from Mt. Sinai (where Moses is said to have received the ten Commandments from God who at the time was disguised as a burning bush), arriving in the evening had time to explore the three major areas—the Pit at the subterranean level, the Queen's Chamber in the middle, and the King's Chamber at the highest point. The remarkable chamber is a thirty-four-foot by seventeen-foot room with a seventeen-foot-high ceiling made entirely of rose granite blocks. There are one-hundred-and-one blocks and nine beams that comprise the room.

Our small band of spiritual seekers held hands and sang a "peace mantra" (Tina Turner rocks a version of it here: *https://www.youtube.com/watch?v=6XP-f7wPM0A* although it didn't sound quite like this) in unison for a few hours around the rose granite box-sarcophagus. The sarcophagus is so big, the box could not have fit through the door, as it weighs 5.75 tons, including the top slab. The whole place is an absolute mystery, and it is said to be unbuildable with today's technology. We took turns lying in the granite bed while those not on the bed maintained a circle and sang with rhythmic voices.

When it was my turn, I scrambled into the rose quartz granite box and quickly found my center. In my mind's eye, I saw a three-dimensional symbol that contained a thought form, or possibly it was a thought form with a corresponding shape. A shimmering celadon green egg, divided into three-dimensional puzzle pieces, appeared in front of me. A voice in my head, or rather information telepathically communicated to my mind, spoke to the core of my being. I then "knew" that the green puzzle egg was the shape of the universe as God had created it. My later research revealed that the "cosmic world egg" or "egg-shaped universe" is creation imagery in our most ancient civilizations. In Egyptian mythology, the first primordial being is hatched from the cosmic universal egg. In the ancient holy books of India called the Vedic scriptures, it is written in Sanskrit that the universe is shaped like an egg called *Brahmana* (ब्रह्माण्ड) (derived from *"Brahmi"* (ब्रह्म) meaning "expanding cosmos" plus the word *"anda"* (अण्ड) meaning "egg").

PERU, THE AMAZON JUNGLE
AND MY MOTHER-IN-LAW

My adventures in Peru led me on the Inca trail to Machu
Picchu and Lake Titicaca, both locations which I suspect are
some sort of electro-magnetic anomalies, vortexes or earth
energy hotspots. My journey into the Amazon jungle was
the first time I realized I could read minds and thoughts. In
retrospect, all these experiences awakened my latent ability to
perceive information outside myself, an ability I believe resides
in all of us. This foundation of intuitive skill development was
the preparation for my communication with the spirit world.
But who would have thought experiencing the spirit world
would be strongest through my mother-in-law?

When she stopped by our home one evening, Eve wore a peach
chiffon blouse with pearl earrings, the ones my husband had
saved his allowance to give her. He can't remember now if his
gift was for Mother's Day or her birthday. This was the first
time I had met her and two hours flew by. The only thing
was ... Eve had died in 1976, over three decades ago.

I first perceived an energy density in our living room as my
husband and I chatted after dinner about his mother and
remembered her. I could feel a solid personality and loving
nature. Was this someone I knew? My husband thought
possibly this was his mother, because the peach blouse
and earrings were accurate descriptions of actual favorites
Eve wore regularly. I certainly wasn't sure at first that I was
communicating with his mother—but when I drew a picture of
the unusual buttons and texture of the garment I'd seen her
wearing in my mind's eye, my husband was convinced. My
drawing was a near-perfect rendering of her favorite dress, the
one she had been buried in. He admitted later that he'd said
a silent prayer for her to send a sign he couldn't miss, and the

drawing I did was all he needed. The experience touched my husband's heart, and he knew unequivocally that his mom was still with him. It meant the world to him. A feeling of deep love washed over me, but from an unfamiliar perception . . . there was a warmth and appreciation for me as a wife to a son and as the mother to grandchildren. I knew she was thanking me from the other side.

My perception expanded, and I began utilizing more of my natural intuitive ability. I had been working with my intuition

CLOSED MIND • OPEN MIND
THE CHOICE IS YOURS

for a long time, but this experience broadened the spectrum. There is no map of the afterlife, but my research was drawing me to both ancient and world cultures as well as to scientific discoveries.

My conclusion?

Most cultures throughout history have embraced the cycle of life and death in terms of one journey with different stages—for example, the butterfly/chrysalis metaphor. Cutting-edge science has said we are in constant flux and we're mostly a vibrating wave containing little matter, and that consciousness is radically important, seeming to affect every aspect of our lives.

But I struggled with the idea of talking to dead ancestors—what would the neighbors say if they knew?

INTUITION AND THE TABOO AGAINST KNOWING WHAT YOU KNOW

THE TABOO AGAINST COMMUNICATING WITH ancestors and animals had kept me in check in my conventional suburban neighborhood. I had hidden my gift of intuition for fear of social rejection and the thought of embarrassing my family. I anticipated harsh judgment and preferred to fit seamlessly inside my wonderful community. Only my clients and a handful of friends knew I had a developed sixth sense, and I rarely used the word "psychic" because of the stigma.

Nonetheless, word spread about my intuitive readings and drawings. I'd scribble out images for a client. Sometimes an exact portrait of the person or animal in question would emerge. A diverse group of people began seeking me out with a variety of questions and requests about relationship issues, spirit communication with loved ones on the other side, resolving unfinished business and regrets, dealing with grief, soulmate queries, animal communication, horse whispering, and communication with kids who couldn't talk or use sign language (my pro bono work). Health, legal, and financial professionals were interested in looking at work questions and, of course, there were those who were simply curious. A significant portion of people were just "stuck" on their path, and only needed a different perspective to move on in their lives.

My "intuitive practicum" was developed during this time and after a while, I amassed a collection of remarkable stories and drawings from my intuitive investigations. I felt a yearning to share the wisdom I had gleaned from my clients, both human and animal. Kara was the first person I began writing about. Her story led to writing another one, which then led to yet another, and after some time I had a collection of fascinating encounters I wanted to share. But being a shy and private person, I was reluctant to step out of the "intuitive" closet. My fear of other people's opinions caused me to clip my own wings. This girl wouldn't fly. Publishing felt out of the question. My subconscious must have missed the memo though, because I began to have a recurring dream: I was struggling to catch an airplane, but regardless of my heroic attempts, the flight always took off without me. Panic would wake me and I knew I was missing something BIG in my life. Nothing inspired me to create more than using my intuition. The more I followed my heart's desire, the less I missed the plane. Once I decided to go public with the remarkable stories of animal intelligence and "love that never dies", I finally made the flight.

© JANE DE FOREST

COMPASSION

© JANE de FOREST

DELPHIC ORACLE
1400 BCE

THE BACKSTORY

FOR THOSE OF YOU WHO are meeting me for the first time, a few words of introduction are needed. I'm a classically trained artist who attended the Rhode Island School of Design and Interlochen Arts Academy. I have painted murals in many grand homes, and my paintings or giclee prints hang in the collections of the amazing Jane Goodall, Martin Sheen, and Joan Borisanko. Creativity bubbles out of me and is connected to how I see the world. In my years of doing guided visualization with kids and as a professional artist, I've developed a system for understanding and communicating concepts beyond words.

BEING A PROFESSIONAL INTUITIVE

BEING A PROFESSIONAL INTUITIVE IS a dream I have had since I was a little girl. I would watch fortune tellers and tealeaf readers with a deep sense of awe . . . I too wanted to possess the psychic superpower they seemed to command. It cannot go unnoticed that my parents named me Sibyl but later decided on Jane to honor my beloved grandmother. In the ancient world the Sibyls were a class of intuitively gifted women who communicated with the Gods and Goddesses that comprised their pantheon. Kings and generals consulted these oracles for their intuitive insights before any military campaigns and major decisions, while seekers from every walk of life looked for guidance on everyday concerns.

Painting in my art studio, I would naturally enter a sort of timeless place where my imagination and intuition overlapped. In this state of expanded consciousness, which I called "the zone," I produced my most beautiful work. As a child, I spent many of my days in imaginary places, and my creative and brilliant family encouraged magical thinking in innumerable ways. It was also a way to cope with a difficult home life.

As an adult, I expanded and developed the "zone" through study with teachers and persistent practice. Sacred locations also had an unexpected effect in boosting my capabilities, by creating a kind of "opening" experience.

When I teach, or give people assignments after a reading, I try to tease out their creativity. My primary tools for helping people get unstuck are guided visualization and art. Focusing our mind and creating art with our hands, in a purposeful or prayerful way, can help us get out of our own way. For the many people who get stuck in the rational mind and forget the creative person inside, these are the first steps that make the important journey to self-mastery a little easier.

I was brought up in a highly intellectual and artistic family that valued the arts, literature and ancient history. My mother is a courageous and brilliant woman, an eccentric artist, classical musician, and was a management consultant and

WISDOM IS MORE
IMPORTANT THAN STUFF

FEATHER
OF TRUTH

GOLD

© TARA DE FOREST

art history professor at a time when women in the workplace were an anomaly. Fascinated by indigenous cultures, she traveled like an anthropologist to the outer reaches of Mexico in the 1970s, 80s and 90s, meeting important shamans and mask makers. Out of concern for my mother, I persuaded the red-haired elder to live with us. She was reluctant to move from the cultural center of Chicago to what she considered the outback of the Pacific Northwest. Moreover, we just did not get along. She was my nemesis and the journey to healing our relationship was tantamount to my climbing Mt. Kilimanjaro, and frankly one of my greatest rock-star moments—for both of us. I consistently, well pretty consistently, chose to open my heart instead of holding on to acrimony like a precious jewel. And as these things go, my open heart was returned ten-fold, as having her share our lives has been a blessing in more ways than I can count.

My illustrious grandfather, Abby, had a brilliant Jewish mind. He studied philosophy at Johns Hopkins University at the height of the Depression. Most of his relatives had been wiped out in Austria during the war, and he studied the Bible's origins, hoping to understand how religious ideas justified bloodshed for millennia. *Gilgamesh*, the epic poem and *The Complete Dead Sea Scrolls* and *The Lost Books of The Bible* were on his library shelf next to mounds of *New York Times'* clippings on the floor.

Jane, my grandmother, could read and write Egyptian hiero-glyphics and was one of the original docents at the Oriental Institute of the University of Chicago. She would drag me through the famous museum, pointing out amazing artifacts like the forty-ton sculpture of a human-headed winged bull from Assyrian King Sargon II's palace. My grandparents had a deep affinity for the ancient world and spoke nine languages between them. As brilliant as they were though, God did not fit into their intellectual worldview, although, inexplicably, we were Episcopalians.

I was raised to respect deep knowledge, but as a child I couldn't read the books on my grandparents' shelves. Severe dyslexia had rendered me unable to crack the code of "book learning", leaving me extremely discouraged and frustrated. In retrospect, I realize that, as a result, I opened up to acquiring knowledge in other ways, just as the visually impaired develop a heightened sense of sound or smell. I would "feel out" a situation and pick up information and get images. I suspect this was the prelude to the development of my intuition, my sixth sense.

I later trained with Louise Hauck, an internationally known psychic, as her first apprentice in her now successful program.

Vipassana meditation helped relieve my anxiety and led me to Buddhism, Kundalini Yoga, and tantric breath. When I was ready, my most important teacher appeared . . . a Lakota medicine woman whose body pushed 400 pounds. She wore a smear of hot pink lipstick that landed more or less inside the lines. I didn't recognize her at first as being enlightened because I was waiting for someone who looked like the Dalai Lama, or at least Ram Dass, but she turned out to be my most pivotal teacher and the one to whom I owe my greatest gratitude.

INSPIRED BY THE DOVE

THE FINAL PUSH TO FOLLOW my dream came on the wings of a dove. At our daughter's college graduation, we sat in a sea of umbrellas in the shadow of Thomas Jefferson's magnificent rotunda. The University of Virginia was releasing myriads of graduates into the world. Keynote speaker, Rita Dove, sang her words in rhythmic cadence, savoring syllables like dark chocolate. The powerful message she offered was directly for me, I was sure, mainly because she nailed my struggles specifically: my inner yearning for life's authentic work and a need to follow my spiritual path. The poet laureate and Pulitzer Prize winner's simple wisdom pierced my soul. Her lyrical voice cut through my defenses and spoke directly to a deep place inside.

She said:

1. Life is short.

2. Don't put yourself in a box.

3. There's a reason certain people, places, books, ideas, etc. "make our ears stand up"; always follow what attracts you.

Rita Dove had been triumphant in overcoming obstacles much greater than mine and had dusted the world with magnificence. Her creative spirit was too huge to squish down into a box, she allowed herself to grow and blossom beyond the confines of limiting ideas. As I stood on that famous lawn, I watched her undulating crystalline energy field with my eyes closed. I saw luminous trails emanating far beyond her physical body. I felt an overwhelming wave of gratitude. *The world is a better place because she is in it,* I thought.

Life is short, had I put myself in a box?
What attracted me?
What ideas and places made my ears stand up?
Had I really done what I'd come to do?
There is only so much time.
Regrets?
Well, a few . . . yes.

The reality of my limited sojourn on Earth hit hard.

© TARA DE FOREST

All that we are is a result of what we have thought.

BUDDHA

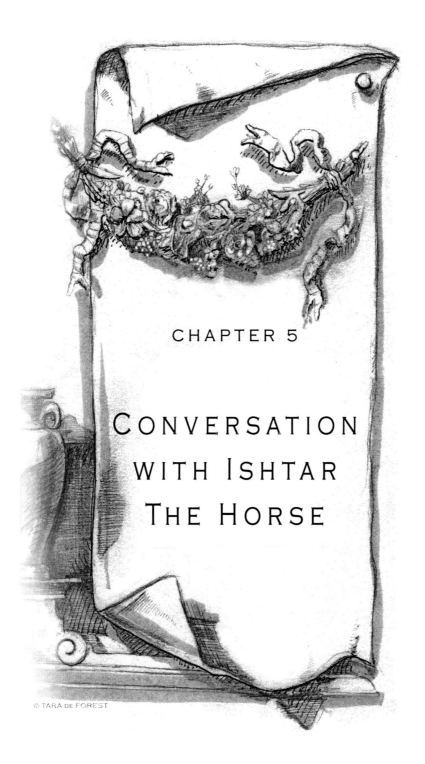

CHAPTER 5

CONVERSATION WITH ISHTAR THE HORSE

© TARA DE FOREST

My Conversation With Ishtar The Horse

The names and location in this story have been changed. I've placed the story in some of my favorite places in the Pacific Northwest, and I've included a letter from the horse's human at the end.

Wind of Heaven is that which blows between a horse's ears.

ARABIAN PROVERB

ANIMALS ARE SOME OF MY favorite clients, and work with them is one of the most gratifying things I do (besides working with children). Their pure energy and open hearts make accepting an offer to help an animal a joy, so I was looking forward to this reading. Animals have so much to teach us, and many of us count our pets as high-ranking family members. Communicating with the "four-legged" feels like a noble calling to me, but animals are at a marked disadvantage in a world of two-legged creatures because most people underestimate their intelligence or don't believe they can telepathically communicate with animals.

When I was invited to help an ailing horse by communicating directly with her, I was delighted and nervous. I'd had previous contact with horses, so I was not completely unfamiliar with the concept of trans-species communication, but horse whispering was not my specialty. Realizing I needed all the help

© TARA DE FOREST

I could get, I asked for my spiritual equine guide (assuming I had one) to help me interpret the messages of a stately horse named Ishtar.

As I pulled into Ishtar's stables, I was impressed. They looked well kept and well run. Claire waited for me with a warm smile. She is a sweet woman with a kind heart and gentle manner, who loves her horse with depth and passion. Claire's life reads like a tragic novel, but no darkness can dim her light. An optimistic and positive person, she was a pleasure to work with. Being a devout Christian, she had found solace in her religion, and in a way, she also found solace in her relationship with this horse. Ishtar was part of her healing.

Claire seemed relieved to see me and wanted to get right to work. She had tried everything she could think of to get Ishtar to jump, but the horse refused. The animal had become more and more aggressive. Claire was desperate. Was this situation a spoiled behavior problem, was it due to pain, or something else?

We made our way to Ishtar's stall and approached carefully, hoping not to spook her. The powerful horse turned her imposing head to examine me, and her large eyes seemed to penetrate my thoughts. The horse's head felt soft under my hand as I breathed in and centered. Her feelings and images filled my mind. They were clearly non-human.

The quality of an equine is solid, earthy, sweet, honest and simple, with the intelligence of a five-year-old child, give or take. Yet there is maturity and sexuality and, if the horse has not been abused, it has a sense of humor. The world from a horse's perspective is shaped by a rich variety of smells, an awareness of its surroundings, and an ever-present state of high alert. I am not sure if a horse can see color, but I believe they have a perception of hue because they seem to communicate the color of such things as sky and trees.

Claire lives in Bend, Oregon, which she considers one of the most beautiful places on the planet. The town has art galleries, interesting restaurants, concerts and Shakespeare in the park. Bend is a mecca for sports enthusiasts, bikers, hikers, skiers, mountain climbers and white-water rafters. Not to mention sportsmen who love fishing the pure waterways and lakes.

I had taken Highway 26 on Mount Hood's mountain pass from Portland the day before in order to meet with Claire and Ishtar. The mountain is really a volcano (you can't fool me, I'm from Chicago) and is one in a string of volcanoes that make up the "Ring of Fire", a major area of the Pacific Ocean that contains over 450 volcanoes—seventy-five percent of the entire world's volcanoes.

© JANE DE FOREST

MT. HOOD OREGON

Known as Wy'east by the Multnomah Indian tribe, the conifer forests are thick and dense on the foothills. At the timberline, only rock and glaciers push up to the 11,000-foot pinnacle.

Traveling down from the pass's almost 5,000-foot elevation, I passed through the Warm Springs Indian Reservation where the landscape gave way to the arid high desert. Scrub sage with red soil covered the gentle slopes and the Cascade mountain range revealed the jagged basalt peaks of the Three

Sisters' mountains. About sixteen-million years ago, huge volcanic eruptions in Washington, Oregon and Idaho produced enormous volumes of molten lava that flowed like water as far west as the Pacific Ocean. As I drove along, I focused on the crystal blue sky that seemed to stretch from one edge of the Earth to the other. An eagle circled overhead and I felt grateful for this exquisite moment as I pulled up to the stables..

I turned my attention to the task at hand: to talk to a horse. Well actually, talking to a horse isn't the difficult part; hearing what the horse has to say is the part that's a bit trickier.

A supple eight-year-old bay mare with a white star on her forehead, Ishtar was smart and mischievous, but also a bit overindulged. Claire had struggled with Ishtar's spoiled behavior and this was exactly why she had inquired about my services. We were trying to determine what would correct Ishtar's lack of interest in jumping and her general reluctance to follow commands. It turned out there was a good explanation for why she wasn't interested in jumping.

The reason was her leg: jumping hurt her.

Closing my eyes, I prayed. "I ask Creator to guide my words and actions to help me do my best work." I imagined white Christ-light and a feeling of unconditional love surrounding

us—we were completely enveloped. I invoked four archangels and asked them to stand in the four corners of the stall. Immediately I saw them there in my mind's eye.

I let Ishtar know my intentions were peaceful by cultivating genuine love and affection for the horse in my mind-body. I imagined holding my dog, Shaman, in my arms when she was a cute puppy. I pictured the feeling as light and sent it from my heart to Ishtar's heart in an infinity-shape. The connection took a few minutes and I began to feel the animal opening up to me.

As I settled in to "read" the magnificent creature, the first thing I "saw" was a tall slender woman with big jewelry and a sad heart. Then I felt pain in my stomach . . . then my front right leg . . . then I smelled fresh air.

This was going to be a wild ride without my even leaving the stables.

Listening intently, I created space in my mind, allowing me to be receptive to the animal's information. Images began to materialize, then feelings arose in conjunction with them.

"The horse is telling me her front right leg hurts. That's why she wasn't interested in jumping," I reported. "She is showing me a sock for her leg that is super-tight. Could that be right?"

"There is a type of boot that would help her if her leg was in pain—yes that makes perfect sense. I'll have the stable hand take care of it," said Claire.

Unfortunately, there was a miscommunication and the stabilizing sock/boot that Ishtar wanted was never fitted. A few weeks after our session, another rider took the horse jumping and her leg blew out. Claire despaired about the animal's suffering and lamented that now the horse would never jump again.

I got the impression the elegant older woman was important—the horse seemed genuinely to like her, and at the same time I could feel the authentic affection this older woman felt for the horse. In truth, I intuited this woman adored Ishtar.

Incredibly, Ishtar described this previous owner's emotional state; the horse showed me (through feelings) that the woman's love for her had made it difficult for her to say goodbye when Ishtar was sold. The horse knew only that she had to leave her owner, having, of course, no concept of money or ownership. Consequently, she did not understand being sold, or the reason she had to leave the nice elegant lady and the stables she called home.

Ishtar was somehow also aware the woman had lost her husband, or a male child, or both. The image I received was of a woman surrounded by sadness, with her head hung low, carrying a burden that resonated with male energy. What was most amazing was that the horse was correct, as Claire corroborated immediately.

"That's true. She was an elegant older lady who wore big chunky jewelry. She was heartbroken at having to sell her horse after she'd had a fall and could no longer ride her. Yes, her husband divorced her, leaving her abruptly for a younger woman. That was a difficult time for her," Claire reported.

 "Now I see a small meadow encircled by pine trees. The grass is sweet and Ishtar loves this place. Are you familiar with the location?" I could taste sweet grass in my mouth.

"Yes! That was Ishtar's old stomping ground, and she DID love the place! That was the elegant lady's stables, I mean, the

© JANE DE FOREST

© JANE DE FOREST

previous owner's," said Claire.

"Now I see a meadow on a cliff overlooking a river. The sky is blue and I smell fresh air. I can see Ishtar is happy at this place."

"Her current pasture overlooks the Deschutes River," said Claire.

"The horse is giving me the awareness of birds flying. Some are noisy, well, downright raucous . . . oh, and big too, enormous."

That's curious, I thought. I heard a loud bird. *Is the bird a hawk or an eagle? Screeching? But they aren't that loud*, I told myself. I waited a moment, hoping something would come to me. Claire and I looked at each other and a light bulb went off above both of our heads simultaneously.

"AIRPLANES!" we said and laughed. The stables were on a flight path to a busy airport. I was floored. *A horse understanding all this!* I was astonished and full of wonder at how astute, how intelligent, this horse was. This in-depth conversation with an animal felt both humbling and inspiring.

I centered and tried to merge with the horse's consciousness. A feeling of affection came over me but the emotion was different, more like a powerful affinity, a deep friendship, resembling camaraderie. Then I saw an image of a light-colored horse in a green field on a sunny day. That horse conveyed male energy.

Was I interpreting this correctly? Could this be how horses care about each other? This is extraordinary . . . am I experiencing "horse love?"

"I think there is a horse that Ishtar likes or maybe loves, in a horsey kind of way. The energy feels male, and the horse looks lighter in color. Oh yes, and feels massive, too."

Claire looked stunned. Ishtar was "attached" to an eighteen-hand grey Dutch Warmblood gelding. The two were favorite companions and enjoyed each other's company and rubbed noses, which might be horse kisses. A huge meadow encircled by evergreens was a favorite place for the horses on warm sunny days. Ishtar was separated from her friend when Claire switched barns, but as fate would have it, the two were reunited at the stables they both now shared.

"I have a photo of their foreheads touching, forming a perfect heart shape, with Mt. Bachelor in the distance," Claire said.

With all of the intrigue, I had been distracted from the fact that I was standing with my eyes closed in the small, enclosed space with a 1,200-pound animal that could, at any time, crush me, or at least do some serious damage. Claire was completely comfortable with this giant beast and didn't seem bothered, but I certainly didn't think being in such close proximity was a good idea. I tried to act as nonchalant as possible, slipping behind the other side of the half-sized stable door.

From my position there, I could see an illuminated line, a vein perhaps, behind Ishtar's right eye, and an aching on that side of her face. Headaches related to barometric pressure? Her gut felt upset, but otherwise I sensed her spine was strong, and I felt "healthy" when I scanned her body. Claire wondered if that was why the horse had been shaking her head and why her stomach had seemed sensitive to the touch.

"There might be another reason Ishtar has abdominal pain. She is telling me about a young woman, a teenager perhaps, who rides her. She hurts her with her feet. This girl has a closed heart to the horse. She chews gum, or something with her mouth, and has brown hair."

Claire was visibly upset at the idea of someone hurting her beloved horse. She later showed me a picture of a brown-haired teenage girl with braces who rode Ishtar at a weekly lesson. She wondered if the spurs she wore were digging into Ishtar's belly.

Claire was overwhelmed by the reading, but considering the magnitude of the experience, she was doing pretty well. I was confident she would remedy the situation with the hurtful rider soon.

MY EXPERIENCE AS A "psychic horse whisperer" had been relatively limited. I decided to improve my skills, so at a local stable, I made the rounds, visiting stalls and taking notes, recording the images, feelings and events the horses communicated to me. Some facts were verifiable because of the length of time a horse had lived at the stable and how much information previous owners had provided. There were plenty of details that could not be proved though, and some details were slightly off, such as the exact number of years the horse had lived at that stable. For example, a horse told me he arrived at the stable when he was four years old, yet the correct number was five. Either my reading was off, or the horse measured time differently.

© TARA DE FOREST

I have found that horses have qualities similar to dogs, with respect to their essence, intelligence and energy field. Within each species, there are also variances among individual animals. A number of horses have told me about "bad men" who punched, cursed and spit on them, apparently in the racing world. Horses don't seem to be resentful or bitter, but they do remember insults and pain and can have the equivalent of psychological human problems. Horses love in a way that is different from human love—a sort of diffuse affectionate bond, not the broad spectrum and depth of feeling that humans have.

Claire wanted to address an issue that was bothering her about her horse's behavior.

"Jane, another reason I contacted you was that I've been having difficulty with Ishtar's aggression about her stall and space. Any ideas?"

I sensed the reason was "pampering" and suspected the previous owner spoiled the animal. Claire admitted that the woman had indulged Ishtar because she felt guilty for riding her infrequently. With that, we'd found the root of the problem.

Now I wanted to give Claire some concrete suggestions so I asked the horse what displeased her. Ishtar showed me an image of a horse facing the corner, like an old-fashioned schoolhouse "dunce" punishment. If Claire tried to discipline the horse in this way, I could see how things would work out successfully. But I also saw that encouraging the horse would work if Clair was judicious with treats.

Ishtar also felt lonely, and a little bored.

"Well," I said, "about the behavior problems: this horse is spoiled and she still wants rewards more than the occasional "atta girl." Rewards are important to her, but she also needs discipline. I 'saw' her head being held in the stall corner to break her of bad habits. Does that sound like a possible training technique? If so, I'm getting that you should be through the worst in two months if that's stopped. Also, Ishtar asked that she be visited more often. All the barn activity has often left her standing alone, with no one coming FOR HER! She is lonely, and that is, in part, why she is mad at you when you arrive.

"She is showing me a barn stall with music playing. She's asking for music, but I don't think she likes the country-western type. I feel she'll like something more like classical. I'm thinking more Mozart and less Merle Haggard. Oh and by the way, she LOVES you Claire, in a horsey kind of way! You are important to her and she thinks you belong to her. She doesn't understand that you own her."

What a different world this would be if we could respectfully honor animals. They have spirits and want to be loved. In return, they love and serve us.

Heading back home, I felt a sense a satisfaction and awe as I reflected on the healing power of animals that want to please and love us unconditionally. In a way they are guides for us that happen to speak a different language.

Life is good, the simple things . . .
each moment is exquisite.

"The grace of God
is found between the saddle and the ground."
IRISH PROVERB

A LETTER FROM CLAIRE

Dear Jane,

I can't thank you enough for your time and energy in doing this reading of my horse. I am just amazed. As a human, I want to hear horses speak, but I just stare unknowingly into their large captivating eyes and am left to wonder. Through you, Ishtar expressed words and memories, and told us about her leg pain and even loneliness and her desire to be visited more often. Ever since you did the horse whispering reading, I have made a new commitment to ride every day, to check in on her, and even to drive to the stables after hours and say goodnight. She seems much happier.

Because of you, Jane, I've opened my heart and love Ishtar more than I ever thought possible. That love has helped me accomplish what I thought couldn't happen after so much pain in my life. I have healed.

Jane, you showed me that my horse is a reflection. Thank you for sharing her thoughts with me. I am astounded. I can now breathe her scent and embrace her heartbeat more completely, knowing her words and hearing her thoughts. You opened her soul to me and shared her ideas, opinions and even her needs. What a gift! I will be forever grateful.

Sincerely,
Claire

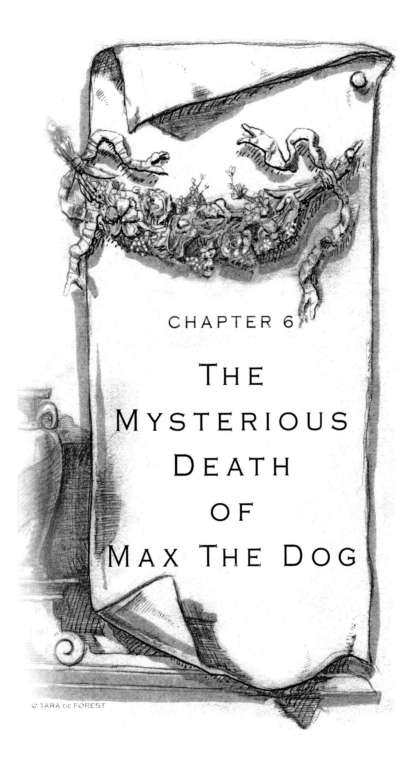

CHAPTER 6

THE
MYSTERIOUS
DEATH
OF
MAX THE DOG

© TARA DE FOREST

THE MYSTERIOUS DEATH OF MAX THE DOG

In this true story the location is Friday Harbor on San Juan Island in the archipelago of seven hundred-ish islands in the Northwest corner of Washington State. Oh, and names are changed too.

ANNA WAS ANXIOUS TO FIND out what had happened to her dog, which had died under mysterious circumstances a few months earlier. I was dubious about my ability to locate accurate details, but was determined to try.

In her mid-thirties with a voluptuous figure, an exquisite face and cascading hair, Anna was ravishing. A number of colorful and elegant tattoos peaked out from under the soft fabric of her clothes.

Anna preferred to remain single. Many of her friends had married after college and were now divorcing; her life was uncomplicated by comparison. Even though there was no shortage of interested men, Mr. Soulmate had not yet arrived.

But Anna had a family of sorts with her three dogs and they all lived in a comfortable house with a tidy yard.

I sat at her kitchen table, with the Northwest light of early July streaming in. Outside her windows are sweeping views of the Pacific Ocean in Friday Harbor. San Juan Islands was a mountain range before the great flood about 10,000 BCE, now they are seven-hundred-ish islands. But it was time to focus on my client . . . I glanced down at my drawing paper and pencil.

I explained that in intuitive consultations, finding a person "energetically" was essential before I could proceed with anything else. I asked Anna to repeat her name three times and then located her in the "timeless place" of my mind's eye. Her energy field was strong yet delicate, lifting upward to heaven, with a wide cord descending back to Earth. I knew this represented Anna's vital connection to nature, and meant that she was stronger than she believed. I also confirmed the instant affinity between us I'd felt upon meeting her, and that had made it easy to sense her energy.

I closed my eyes and intoned my regular invocation prayer: "Surrounding us with the golden white light of Christ consciousness, invoking Mother-Father God, Great Spirit, and the Creator of all things, I ask the archangels Uriel, Raphael, Michael and Gabriel, the four directions, our higher selves, God self, and spirit guides to be present." Then I asked that I be provided with the highest, purest information from the canine realm, for me to receive, and for the client to hear. I thanked "The Big Guy" for the gift of second sight and for the opportunity to be of service. I then asked that my personality self, or ego-self, step aside and not interfere, as my ego-mind can be quite clever. I always send anything negative "to the light" and protect myself completely and entirely—nothing but the light is allowed here. I imagine a white light surrounding me, a root growing down into the ground, and my "crown chakra" at the top of the head, opening to the Creator. I have taken bits from other prayers and inspirations to create this prayer, and it works for me. It is organic and it changes—in fact, it has evolved over the twenty years I have been doing readings.

I had meditated for about an hour before her appointment, using basic mind-clearing techniques. I focus on my breath, notice my body move with each inhalation, and acknowledge an electric energy traveling up and down my spine. To elevate my consciousness, I allow loving thoughts to fill my mind until I feel safe and expansive. Then I imagine my heart connecting to all living things, creating a luminous web of light Once I've achieved a warm-hearted emotional level and a higher state of mind, I can more easily access psychic information.

Sketching Anna's heart chakra on the drawing paper in front of me, I saw that the light of her chakra veered way off to the right, circled around, then returned to her chest. I could tell Anna was hurting. A rendering emerged on my paper. First I

MAX COMES BACK

saw Anna's energy, and then that of Max, her dog. The information was all coming quickly.

Anna deeply loved her dog. Max's death had broken her heart and she was suffering greatly. Although the details of Max's demise were sketchy, the loss of her four-legged companion was brutally real. I took a moment to open my own heart in compassion for Anna's loss because sometimes the frequency of grief is intense.

"Anna, I got some impressions of Max before you arrived that are dovetailing into some additional images. Please let me know if what I'm describing is accurate."

I explained that it was important to nail down some specifics for my own edification, to make sure I was, in fact, communicating with Max the dog. It is easy enough to say, "Your dog loves you and you will see him again," but it is a completely different matter to come up with undeniable facts that are beyond the realm of everyday knowledge.

My intuitive impression of Max was of a bright, obedient, loyal and happy dog. He was quite clear to me, with a wagging tail. Two more dogs appeared, in my mind's eye—one with long hair and another smaller dog. I sensed a strong pressure on the left side of Max's head and left paw. My 6B pencil sketched quickly. There was a lot to tell Anna, and I felt optimistic that the spirit of Max and I would be able to help her.

"I feel pressure on the left side of his body and on his head and paws, too. I have a sensation of concrete or metal. A car may have hit him, but whatever happened, there was a terrible impact for sure. As I enter his mind, I feel it is hard for Max to pick up his head . . . it may be fractured," I said.

Anna's jaw dropped open and then she was overwhelmed by

emotion. "Yes, that's absolutely accurate." Something struck him on the left side of his body. He had three broken ribs on the left and possibly a fractured skull. He died from his injuries, but it's a mystery as to how this occurred. Do you see anything? I have to know. It's eating me up inside. I just feel sick about it," she said, with tears in her eyes.

I saw a man, older, maybe in his fifties, with dark salt-and-pepper hair. I sensed this man lived close to Anna. I felt dark, low, thick energy and saw an ugly reddish color. I sensed violence . . . then the energy felt cold, like steel.

Hmm, I don't like this place much. It feels terrible, actually: dark, dirty and with a smell of drugs.

I quickly distanced myself from close psychic proximity to this person's consciousness and energy. There was little that was redeeming about this man, and "hellish" was the feeling of his physical space and mindset. Frankly, it felt like some hell-like places I've encountered right here on Earth. Then I felt a stronger presence from the dog. The warmth and intelligence from the spirit of this deceased canine enveloped me.

Dogs have a warm, affectionate quality, similar to humans in that way. They are loving, open, generous, intelligent and accepting (for the most part—that is, as long as the dog has not been mistreated). Max was linked to his owner, and I could see a palpable connection between them in the form of a thick luminous cord. I suspected these two had been together in previous lifetimes.

Images and non-linear information flooded my conscience in double time. I resonated with a sense of responsibility and concern that felt non-human. I concluded the dog's spirit was expressing his genuine concern for Anna. Next, I sensed a clear barrier, like a tempered glass wall between the evil, nefarious energy of the "bad man" and me.

I knew Max was trying to tell me something. I perceived a certain amount of dread as I approached, and wondered if it was a warning. An awareness that any action would come to no good end-stopped me for a minute.

Was this an instruction to keep my distance? Now it was my turn to be amazed! Could this be the spirit of the dog warning his human, Anna, in the physical world? Can this happen? Are dogs that smart?

My hair stood on end, as an uneasiness welled up in my stomach and coursed through my body, sending an elec-tro-magnetic pulse shooting up my spine. The event really did feel like murder! Now I understood that Max the dog had died of the wounds most probably inflicted by the "bad" man with the salt and pepper hair.

I was relatively confident that Max was attempting to tell Anna NOT to try to figure out who had killed him. He was advising Anna that she must not get involved in the "story of who had hurt/murdered him" by showing me in pictures that she should not enter the "bad man's" toxic story. Pursuing retribu-tion would certainly result in bitterness at best and possibly even put Anna in danger's way in a worst-case scenario.

Well, that's pretty amazing, I thought. A dog giving his former owner advice—it seemed beyond the realm of possibility. But the truth of the matter was, I was sitting in my office, commu-nicating with the spirit of a dog and translating a canine message to his bereft and amazed human owner.

I love what I do.

Anna told me the genteel elderly woman next door had moved to assisted living, leaving the house to her wayward relatives. Within short order the charming bungalow had been transformed into a meth house, inhabited by a variety of addicts and transients. Sure enough, Anna had already suspected that her neighbors might have been involved in some way in Max's death, but she had no way of knowing . . . that was, until our visit. Anna had called the police when things got too loud. The possibility existed that the "bad man" hurt Max in retaliation for several complaints she had made to law enforcement.

"Anna, as remarkable as this seems, your dog appears to be advising you to move on, sort of like, 'Don't touch this with a ten-foot pole.' I get the strong impression that any action will only cause you more trouble and resentment, if not put you in an even more dangerous situation. Nothing you can do will teach the perpetrators of this crime a lesson, so I guess they'll have to wait for their own karmic delivery. I assure you, the law of karma escapes no one, regardless of what we perceive."

"You're right Jane, that's good advice. I also love that it's from Max. I've learned to let most things go in my life. I don't harbor resentment any more. Too much of my life was wasted on those feelings, and I did a lot of therapy and inner work."

That made sense to me, because when I looked at her energy field it was surprisingly bright, and her vital energy was in full force.

It's my experience that people who choose to let things go, who forgive and move on, have a much healthier life-force or *chi* energy. Anna was a perfect example of how doing your own personal work and keeping a positive attitude affects a person's "now" and impacts the future, too; how the very real energetic "weather" created by our thoughts in turn affects the general atmosphere of the material world around us. What I believe I saw with Anna, and what I often see, are the mechanics of the idea that *we create our own reality.*

"I got an impression from Max of gratitude and how it felt to be adored. Now he's telling me about two other dogs, one with long hair, and another one who is smaller than he is," I said, changing the subject, getting back to focusing on Max.

"What is he saying about them?" she asked, resting her delicate arm and pressing in. "Oh, by the way, I do have two other dogs. One is a husky mix who is quite hairy, and the other one is smaller than Max. You're right."

"Max is only giving me an awareness of these dogs, nothing more," I said, matter-of-factly. "I have learned that my accuracy is higher if I don't draw conclusions and just report what I read intuitively."

Anna looked a little disappointed.

"But Max is returning to the idea of gratitude, and telling me how much he appreciates you and how he really loved your hugging him. He could feel your love and was devoted to you. Max really appreciates how kind you were to him."

Anna had truly loved this animal and the creature had understood that. Interestingly, Max was intelligent enough to feel gratitude and express it.

I took a moment to breathe and allow silence to define our space. An ancient breathing practice called Kundalini from the dusty past of the Indus Valley is my favorite tool for "finding center." I followed my breath from the bottom of my spine up to the top of my head, but my left-brain searched in vain for the next bit of information, so I rested in the awareness of my

© JANE DE FOREST

MAX GETS A HUG
FROM HIS HUMAN

breath instead. By observing my breath without judgment, I stopped trying and allowed myself to just "be." Then I felt something against my leg—pressure and the awareness of Max's energy.

Was he leaning on me?

"I'm pretty certain Max is showing me that he liked to lean on you. Did he used to lean against you and then look up at you with a funny look on his face?" I asked, seeing the dog in my mind's eye as he regarded me with a strange expression.

"Yes Jane, Max was a leaner! That's absolutely right. Most of what you've said is accurate." She looked utterly stupefied. Max, on the other hand, appeared quite pleased with himself, as he puffed up his chest.

I felt like Dr. Doolittle.

By this time Anna had given up testing me and was convinced I was not making this all up. Tears welled in her big blue eyes and smudged mascara colored her cheeks. The reality was starting to soak in: Max was okay. He just wasn't where she could hug him anymore.

"I'm getting the impression he has visited you. Have you felt him leaning against you? He might be trying to let you know he has visited you, or that he might visit you in the future . . . I'm not sure."

Anna's eyes widened. The previous week, she shared, she had spontaneously opened the back door to let the dogs out, but they hadn't run past her into the backyard. The weirdest thing was, there weren't any dogs at her feet! For no apparent reason, she'd felt a pressure and warmth against her leg. Yet, the other two dogs were curled up in the living room, and besides, they weren't leaners. It was Max who used to lean on her leg when he wanted to go outside.

I was getting one last impression from Max, and as he started to fade, I felt the awareness of his damaged body. But I sensed no pain in him, and I observed his spirit detaching from his physical body. Then I saw his body melting into the ground within a large circle, and the circle turned into an ouroboros, the ancient symbol of a snake biting its own tail. An awareness of the cycle of life rushed into my mind. Then I saw the density of Max's spirit and an interconnection with Anna's soul, and realized what this image meant: he was a guardian spirit-animal or animal guide that had reincarnated with her many times.

A little brown and white puppy popped into my head and I could feel the soft fur between my fingers. I drew a line segment and marked it into sections, which is my protocol for measuring linear time; the demarcated time-line lit up somewhere between ten and fifteen years. Max's final communication came through to me in the thought form of a sphere, something like a ball of twine. I unraveled it.

"Okay, Anna, this is a bit of a download. I feel Max was a spirit-dog. Spirit animals are guides and helpers for us and this one has reincarnated with you many times. You have a connection with him, unlike any animal before, and this is likely the reason. He is indicating to me that he felt no pain when he left his body and died." Anna looked relieved. "He's also showing me an idea that he would like to share with you. He's trying to communicate to you the importance of the idea that death is part of the cycle of life. I see the ancient symbol of a snake biting its tale, which symbolizes that life and death are part of the same strand. I remember you said you were

© TARA de FOREST

returning to school to study about the oceans, and this might be connected." I noticed we had reached the point in the reading were people's eyes glaze over and they can't absorb much more.

"I know this sounds incredible, but this is what I am getting: there may be a greater plan here. Max may be a messenger to teach and guide you. It is not uncommon for animals to do this. This may be why Max picked this lifetime to teach you an important lesson to help you on your path, both spiritually and professionally. This experience has deepened your soul's knowledge and you have Max to thank for this important wisdom-teaching. Animals are often some of our most important teachers, if we can open our hearts." I took a breath.

"The last impression I received was of a puppy. The timeline was about twelve years or so down the road. I cannot predict the future, but I can see potentiality. This could mean that Max will reincarnate as a puppy or possibly that he is guiding a special dog to you; but either way it feels extremely positive."

Whew, certainly it had been an exciting hour chatting with the dog, but it takes a lot of psychic energy to maintain the level required to communicate with the other side. I was starting to feel myself closing down.

"Any more questions?"

"Yes, Jane. What do you see about my life?"

"Anna, I want to say you are extremely strong and I see the image of you holding up the Earth. Your positive attitude is helping you in every possible way. I see that you crave children, but I believe they will come to you in a way that is not through your body. I also see the potential of some male

A LETTER FROM ANNA

WHEN A FRIEND REFERRED me to Jane, I didn't know what to expect, but because I was in such a deep state of grief I was willing to try anything. I liked her from the moment I met her and was surprised that Jane was able to tell me detailed information about Max's injuries. This was the kind of information she could only have gotten if she had read the results of the necropsy that followed his death. My session with Jane gave me peace and a path forward, something I would have struggled to find without her help.

The drawing she did for me for the intuitive consultation I have kept and treasured. On it she drew a silhouette and the front-facing portrait of a dog. I never thought the dog portrait looked quite like Max, because the face was too narrow and the ears were too long. Yet I always thought the silhouette looked very much like Max. It wasn't until about a month ago that I looked at it again and realized the dog in the picture looks just like Oliver, my new dog—with a silhouette of Max looking over us.

Anna

energy. There is a handsome man who is looking at you out of the corner of his eye."

"Actually, there is a man at work I have always liked who is getting divorced. Could that be the new man?" Anna said, hopefully.

"I do see that you both are already acquainted and he has been admiring you. Please let me know."

I signed my name and handed her my drawing; our session had run over a good hour or so and it was time to wrap up. There was more to say but we would have to leave that for another time.

I headed out to the town of Friday Harbor, and strolled through the quaint streets and charming shops. I was looking forward to my sea kayaking tour later in the day and hoped to spot some more whales. On the ride over in our small seaplane, a pod of black and white Orcas, popularly called killer whales, appeared crystal clear in the sound. Anna had everything she needed inside her to live her life well. It gave me hope that our planet had another beautiful soul to magnify the light.

About a year later, Anna called to say she had been dating a special someone, but no puppy had appeared on the horizon so far.

Tree Energy

ANIMAL GUIDES, ALSO KNOWN AS spirit animals or totems, have been helping humans for millennia. From the dusty memory of a distant past, our ancestors have been beckoning and enticing the guardian spirit of wild animals by wearing skin, teeth and feathers. Creating art, making offerings and dancing were the way to increase one's personal power by inviting the attributes of a specific animal.

Animal behavior provided crucial information to locating the best hunting sites, allowing for survival of the tribe. Often this information was communicated telepathically, something that allowed for our continuing evolution over most of 200,000 years.

In our modern culture we view animals as autonomous things, as species or as beings with a scientific label. It has been only relatively recently, in evolutionally terms, that humans have conceived of animals as domesticated captives.

The ancients had a different take on the animal world, and there are many indigenous cultures that still keep the old traditions alive today. They believed animals were messengers from the spirit world. Birds often signified the manifestation of the Holy Ghost to Christians in the shape of a white dove or Great Spirit (God); to the indigenous Americans, this spirit came as an eagle.

In many cultures animals are harbingers of impending events, like the white owls in the Harry Potter series. One of my favorite personal communications with my grandfather soon after his death came through as three great horned owls with distinctive ears and five-foot wingspans.

The first was perched on a streetlight the morning my grand-father, Abby, died. The other I encountered during a five-day silent retreat at a tranquil meditation center not long after his journey back to heaven.

After a full day of wrestling with my "monkey mind" on my meditation pillow, I headed out for a walk, solo, amid the surrounding trees. The sun had just set and the old-growth forest was blanketed with ferns. The soft path was leading me deeper when I heard the haunting screech of an owl. The echo sent an electromagnetic pulse up my spine and I shuddered—this was no ordinary owl. In that moment I felt my grandfather's presence.

Before long, the air moved as the owl landed on a branch right in front of me. I looked at the great bird, and it looked at me. With some hesitation I asked the owl, in plain English, if it was Abby. The huge white and brown owl screeched right back at me.

Yes, it's him, it's my grandfather!

But doubt started to set in.

Maybe it wasn't Abby. Maybe I was imagining it, and it was all wishful thinking.

Looking up into its piercing yellow eyes, I said out loud, that if in fact Abby was taking control of the bird, he should make it nod its head. Incredibly, the owl made a strange gesture of bringing its neck down and out in a lowered position a number of times.

Yes! A nod!

A chill up my spine now enveloped me with a physical sensation and every hair on my body seemed to stand at alert. Cougar and black bear are not uncommon here, and the forest was darkening quickly. Yet I felt strangely calm.

I stood there, silently vibrating.

This certainly was the spirit of my grandfather, returning and making it so obvious that I couldn't miss the signals.

Then doubt crept in again and I felt a bit absurd, as if I'd inadvertently ended up in a Monty Python skit.

How could I be sure this was really Abby? Could this be just a coincidence?

"All right then," I said out loud. "If you are really the spirit of Abby, pick up your leg."

The bird ignored me and stood with both feet fastened to the branch. But the connection between me and this great wild bird was tangible. I knew it was more than just an Audubon wildlife sighting. Another great horned owl soon joined the other one, landing on a Douglas fir branch nearby, and then they flew off together. My thoughts wandered to Abby's wife, my grandmother, and I imagined the two of them together in heaven.

When I researched the owl, the serendipities continued. Another name for the great horned owl is a "tiger owl." My grandmother's nickname was "Tiger."

Within the last few years of his life, Abby and I had an important conversation. We agreed that he would send me a sign he had made it home and that there really was a heaven. That sign had come in the form of an owl.

Here is his eulogy that I wrote a short while before:

"The heart knows a thousand ways to speak."
RUMI

Death/Rebirth – In This Life and Beyond
IN HONOR OF MY GRANDFATHER, ABBY IMBERMAN.

ABBY IS NOT EVEN CLOSE to gone—he is with us as we read this. His true nature, that part of him that is eternal, authentic, part of the Divine, is here with us. He is also Home. The angels have taken him to a better place with God, family and many friends. We will see him again.

Many we love have passed, "died" before us: our family, our ancestors, the family of man. They are well, healthy and vibrant in their new form, their authentic selves. Life continues unabated. There is much hope and strength to be derived from the knowledge that nothing can ever really die.

Coming to Earth is like going on a trip—we put on our earthly body, we pack our bags and travel through the varied terrain of a life. Metaphorically, there are beautiful meadows filled with the most exquisite flowers . . . and there are also huge boulders in the path that seem insurmountable. Sometimes life's journey is very short, and sometimes it lasts many years. But when the true self steps out of its earthly garments, it goes Home . . . we go Home. Like returning from a long trip, it is so very wonderful to be in our own home, in our own bed; and so it is to "die" (as we call it) and return home. Rebirth, who we really are, will never die. What dies are only those aspects that are illusions. Like an earth-bound caterpillar inching laboriously along a branch to find just the right spot: it prepares a nub, hangs upside down and creates a space to die to what he was, to give up everything he knew to be "true", to leave the old way, he is getting ready for his transformation. Once protected, he leaves all remnants of caterpillar behind . . . he liquefies. From what was, emerges a completely different being in physical matter, yet the same spirit.

CHAPTER 7

OUCH!
QUIT IT!

© TARA DE FOREST

OUCH! QUIT IT!

*I am deeply grateful to Pixie for allowing me to tell her
story. All names, locations and details are factual.*

*"Fear is the path to the dark side.
Fear leads to anger.
Anger leads to hate. Hate leads to suffering."*

YODA

"OH MY!" I GASPED, covering my private parts.

I'm not entirely unaccustomed to spirit visitors in my
shower, but when that happens, it's a little jarring.
Of course, my attire, or lack thereof, was of no interest to my
uninvited guest. I had a 10:00 a.m. intuitive reading booked
later that morning for a woman named Pixie, a widow who
had lost her husband to cancer about eight years earlier. I
guessed this was Pixie's husband, but I wasn't sure. He was
jumping up and down in my shower, and I figured he must
have something important to say. He was eager, that seemed
clear. Typically, I require about ten minutes or so to get into
the zone, center and say an invocation prayer. A clear message
from the other side, especially in my current state, was out of
the question.

NOTE: Sometimes I get impressions spontaneously, hear words or see spirits, but it is not common. Although I can feel extreme moods or feel potent energy, I try not to pick up people's energy fields. Allowing my intuitive core to open has a whole set of challenges, such as a grocery store visit, for example, because the pain, confusion, worry, etc. of the general public used to make me feel a little sick. The feeling of joy seems to be much less common in people, at least in the U.S.

Eventually I found that good boundaries and protection were a must, and so I am "closed for business" . . . unless I'm not. Protection and blocking the incoming information are as important as opening to the messages.

As I sat with Pixie LaPlante—yes, her real name—on my over-sized couch, we made ourselves comfortable. I glanced out the window as a hawk flew by. *Messenger*, I thought. I wondered if that sign meant this would be an important reading, and as it turned out, it would be one of my favorites. While I enjoyed the specific details that matched up well, more significantly, I loved how the reading ultimately expanded my understanding of the immense power within all of us.

The hawk is an important symbol; it is considered the messenger of the spirit world. The hawk's meaning is: clear inner vision and awaken spiritual awareness. That symbolic message turned out to be most prophetic.

"Please," I said quietly to myself, "let me be of service in the highest and best way." I then followed this with my standard invocation prayer.

A woman in her late fifties, Pixie had wise eyes that sparkled outward from a kind face. Her nickname is quite an accurate description of her true essence. She possesses the quality of a magical fairy and wise elder all wrapped up together. A delightful, magical person, she is someone who will squeal at things most other grownups don't even see. Adored by children and animals, her *joie de vivre* brings joy to most who meet her. However, life has been difficult for Pixie. While she's experienced family challenges, constant money troubles, and other life demands, it has not dimmed her light, even though these trials have taken their toll.

I met Pixie at a class through a local continuing education program she was teaching. When I walked into the portable classroom, I did not realize what an important spiritual teacher I was about to meet. Pixie knew about the ancient art of making medicine from the roots and leaves of plants and trees. The cornucopia of wild food in the forest is her passion and area of expertise. She is respectful to Mother Nature, along with composting, recycling, and always thanking the plants for their medicine and food before harvesting. In return, Mother Earth graciously reveals her secrets and generously provides food and medicine for Pixie.

We settled into the reading and I closed my eyes and said my

© TARA DE FOREST

invocation prayer, and scanned Pixie's body with my mind's eye. Symbolically, I saw her arms and legs cut off, her energy field was truncated and her energy blocked. I sensed the death of her husband had been a tragedy she had not yet recovered from. A big block around her heart chakra had grey, cloudy energy with a solidified opaque mass inhibiting the flow of life-force energy. There are different names for this same energy force in various cultures; *prana, chi,* grace. Modern science is now recognizing this life force as electromagnetic energy and it is a fascinating subject.

I saw more than what I've just mentioned, but I kept the information to myself as I sensed that Pixie was quite fragile and the information needed to be handled delicately. I proceeded cautiously—a hard call, but sometimes if the truth is served up carelessly it can inhibit healing and cause more damage. In this case it could hurt more than it helped.

"I see a block and feel it's connected to a broken heart. There are lots of negative emotions too. You are removed from parts of who you are and have cut yourself off from life. Does that make sense?"

"Yes." Pixie offered me a weak smile.

"The storm clouds on your heart are more than what I would see from a normal wound from the loss of your husband, Jim."

We create our own weather and I can see it around people. Strong feelings, combined with intense thoughts create powerful weather—good or bad—and that in turn affects what we attract to ourselves. Before I could investigate further, Jim made another appearance. Thankfully, this time I was appropriately dressed. In truth, he barged in. I had not yet opened the door to the other side, but there he was, or someone was, anyway. I could feel the density of a spirit and sense strong focus. The energy of this being was energetic and wiry, with a double dose of love and affection.

"There is someone here who showed up earlier," I said, remembering that morning's foreshadowing in the shower. "Was Jim ah, a . . . live-wire?" I asked as carefully as I could.

"You could say that," Pixie offered with a chuckle. "He was the life of the party, and always had me in stitches. I miss him so much."

"My heart goes out to you," I said, knowing that she loved him deeply, I was filled with compassion. She had told me she'd been engaged at fourteen and that they'd been married for almost forty years. Life seems so unfair sometimes. But, I also know life really does make sense from a higher vantage point. With the understanding that we are in a school of sorts, seeming injustices are more palatable. I believe we are here to learn certain lessons that will help us progress on our spiritual path, and that we are here to learn lessons that include unconditional love, compassion, forgiveness and so on. Like a board game, we move along to the next square, and so it goes until we make it to the end of the game.

I was pretty sure I was looking at Jim. "If you come in the Christ light you may stay," my grilling began. "Please tell me something I could not have known previously—something Pixie will understand."

I began to sketch a rectangular house layout on my drawing paper, with a smaller rectangle on the upper left corner.

"There is the house, and at the far left there is a room as you enter in the front door. Inside that room there is a dresser on the far wall to the right as you come in," I reported to her, expressing what the male spirit sent me telepathically, mind to mind.

"In the dresser, there are small disks and they feel like metal, in the second drawer down. They are underneath some clothes and they are important to you. Does this make any sense?" I asked with my eyes closed to keep focus.

"That's not right," Pixie said.

I felt a pit in my stomach. *Wow, I must be off today.* I took another look at the vision, and there it was again: same house plan, same room, same dresser, same small round metal disks in the second drawer. *Hmm.*

She kindly offered: "You are seeing the sole family treasure, my coin collection. Dad left it to me," Pixie said. "It *is* in the far left room of my house, the dresser *is* on the far wall; that is accurate. But I moved the coins from the second drawer to the third drawer recently. And, oh, by the way, the collection is under clothes."

I met her gaze as tears welled up in her eyes. There is no way I could have known that information. This confirmed that we were speaking to Jim, her late husband. He had survived death

© JANE de FOREST

PIXIE'S COIN COLLECTION
MERCURY DIME

and here he was, having a conversation with her. What could be better news?

I waited a moment to let the reality of the situation sink in. I have found in my experience that it is merciful to give a person space when reunion with a loved one has been achieved. These can be pivotal, life-changing moments. I have to admit, this is one of my favorite stories because it exemplifies in such a powerful way that love never dies. Their love survived death and so will yours—that is the best news around. But what Jim was about to teach me was one of my most important lessons from the after-life, and it was anything but charming. It was scary powerful!

Once Pixie regained her composure, I continued. "Jim is on one knee with his head hung, begging your forgiveness. I am assuming you know what that is about," I said.

"There were a few things, but the biggie was that Jim broke the contract we agreed to. We were going to finish our life together and be old geezers in rocking chairs. But he left early, and I'm pissed," Pixie explained.

I marveled at the scene I have seen so often when the spirits of the departed try to make amends for past behavior during their time on Earth. It seems to me that it is much better to clean up our mistakes while we are still alive, if we can. It is WAY more difficult to make things right once we have to get our message across through the veil.

I continued. "He is showing me an image of himself with a lot of tiny daggers or small knives sticking out of him." *Hmm, what is this?* I thought. "I see . . . he is bleeding. Any idea why?"

I wasn't sure what I was looking at in my mind's eye, but I watched as a pool of blood collected at his feet. *My, this was a gory reading.* While I didn't much care for it at this point, Jim certainly had my full attention.

"No, not at all," she said.

We had a rather long, awkward pause.

Finally I asked, "Could this be symbolic? You didn't actually stab him, I am assuming. Are you stabbing him in your mind?"

"No, I didn't stab him. But, you could say I have been *back-stabbing* Jim by bad-mouthing him. I do it probably every day 'cause I'm pretty pissed at him," she said.

"He is saying that he messed up in some way; he made a bad mistake. It is none of my business unless you want to share," I said. "He is regretful and apologetic."

A rush of deep emotion came right at me; the color was a dark red-grey. It felt heavy and smelled like remorse.

"Can you forgive him?" I said, repeating a question I seem to ask clients frequently. "He is now being seriously hurt by your lack of forgiveness and anger towards him. Your deeply-felt angry thoughts are impeding his progress on the other side, and are adversely affecting him," I said bluntly. "Forgiveness is the key, in my opinion. If you can forgive him, you will set both yourself and him free."

Pixie burst into tears, and I didn't blame her. I realized that I probably could have done a better job of explaining that! Again, I had been too blunt.

As a matter of fact, she was harboring deep anger and resentment. She did not let more than a day go by without expressing how bitter she was at his audacity for breaking

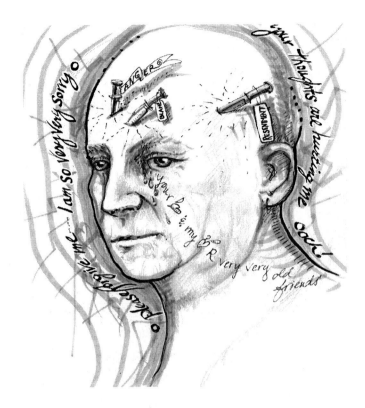

their earthly contract. She was directing focused negative energy at him on a daily basis. The revelation that thoughts transcend the veil between this life and the other side was news to Pixie as well as me. I hadn't realized we could harm spirits on the other side so severely. Certainly, if we could do *that much* harm, think of the good we could actually do. With focused intention, prayer and love, we really are helping our loved ones on the other side.

In a heartbeat, Pixie was able to realize the error in her thinking. Her self-awareness allowed for an honest look. She was willing to change how she thought and I could see it, in real time. Her energy field was no longer truncated or blocked.

Symbolically, Pixie had arms and legs again. Her field was fluid with white light, moving freely. The color was lighter and her crown chakra was open, which is our connection to Spirit.

Our thought patterns are literally like a pattern or three-dimensional array. This field is dynamic and changes with our thoughts in real time. For example, the patterned three-dimensional picture produced by gratitude is beautifully intricate, glowing, and emits a harmonious sound. The three-dimensional array of hatred is ugly and jagged, a dark red-black that emits a dissonance. It's like a matrix around the head, but connected to the body.

The revelation that her late husband, Jim, was not really "gone" and was still around was huge enough, but additionally, the realization that she was powerful enough to adversely affect him on the other side was a lot of information for a Wednesday morning.

Regardless, her choice to think differently and integrate this new information healed her in the twinkling of an eye. She forgave Jim for leaving early to go back home to heaven and for some other things I was not privy to. In doing so, she changed her future. By changing her "now," the universe had opened some doors.

FIVE YEARS LATER

PIXIE'S LIFE STARTED TO IMPROVE. She pulled herself out of a bad rut and is now in a good place and looks radiant and composed. Her effervescent quality brings joy to the people she meets. Most notable is the fact she is no longer scared of her own power because she has "taken it back." Her regular mantra now is, "Thank you for everything being perfect, possible and magical" —and so it is for her. Pixie is a wonderful inspiration.

Out of the blue one evening, I felt the need to call Pixie. As it so happened, this was at the moment she and some family and friends were raising a glass in memory of Jim. He had died that very day, twelve years earlier. I "saw" Jim celebrating with them and knew he was enjoying his party quite a bit. As I focused on his spirit, he made two peace signs.

"By the way, you might want to pour another glass," I said. "Jim is with you at his celebration and he's having a great time. He is trying to get my attention with these funny peace signs at a forty-five-degree angle. Does that make any sense to you?" I asked.

"Glad he's really here," Pixie said. "He liked to flash peace signs. We were hippies, you know. In Jim's last days and right after he died, I would pick an angel card for that day and of course they varied, because there are fifty-two of them. The only card I ever drew in those days was PEACE!"

Love never dies.

A LETTER FROM PIXIE

JIM AND I HAD BEEN together since I was fourteen and he was fifteen. When he died at forty-nine-years old I was hurt, lost and angry. I watched Jim hold on to anger all his life. He held grudges. And as often happens, he got cancer. When my friend Jane said she could invite him to speak to me, I was apprehensive. Jim would say I can be gullible. When Jane described the coin collection and the odd place we used to hide it, I knew she couldn't know this.

Jim wanted to say he was sorry. Like a rose opening slowly, I felt the layers of "I'm sorry" sink in. As the rose unfurled, my heart started to bloom. I felt in my heart each thing he was apologizing for that I had forgiven him about, but he had not forgiven himself.

I felt his heart and the pain he felt when I cursed him for leaving me, breaking our deal.

My healing process got stuck in anger. Now that I could see I was hurting both of us with my anger, I chose to forgive him and let my heart open again. I finished my healing steps and have regained my personal power lovingly and whole-heartedly.

Jane is an amazing aid to healing on both sides of the veil.

Pixie LaPlante Beatty
Washougal, Washington

Pixie and I began to investigate anti-cancer and anti-tumor properties found in nature, which led us to the Oregon Mycological Society where we learned about medicinal mushrooms. Alcohol tincture and tea is an ancient way of extracting medicine from plants and has been used for over 5,000 years for well-being and balance in the East. I encourage you to investigate modern scientific studies on these fungi that have been used medicinally for millennium.

My favorite researcher is Paul Stamets an American mycologist with a powerful TED Talk about the miraculous effects of Turkey Tale mushroom on his mother's cancer. Probably the best place to start is The Mycological Society of America, and of course ... for your own protection, check with your physician before consuming these fungi.

HEALING MUSHROOMS

Turkey Tail Mushroom
CORIOLUS VERSICOLOR/YUN ZHI

This humble mushroom grows in most forests on the planet. Turkey Tail is one of the best researched medicinal mushrooms and some studies show it can reduce the side effects of radiation and chemotherapy treatment. It's an immune builder, and has anti-cancer and anti-tumor properties.

Reishi Mushroom
GANODERMA LUCIDUM/LING ZHI

This mushroom is a very strong anti-oxidant that protects the body from free radicals. It builds the immune system, suppress tumors in people with cancer and has anti-inflammatory properties. It can help with allergies by stopping the release of histamines and can improve the body's liver function.

Cordyceps Mushroom
CHINESE CATERPILLAR FUNGUS/DONG CHONG XIA CAO

This strange looking fungus is the gold standard in medicinal mushrooms. It prolongs the life of white blood cells, has anti-tumor properties, and protects the kidneys from chemotherapy side effects. It is an immune system stimulator that raises T-cells, and is one of the most widely used anti-cancer tonic formulas in Chinese medicine.

Know that all healing forces are within, not without!
The applications from without are merely
to create within a coordinating mental and spiritual force.

EDGAR CAYCE

CHAPTER 8

COUPLES
CONNECTION
FALLING
DEEPER
IN LOVE

© TARA DE FOREST

FALLING DEEPER IN LOVE— RECOGNIZING THE MYSTERY IN YOUR BELOVED

In these true stories, I've changed the locations, names, and some small details.

We're all just walking each other home.

RAM DASS

JULIE AND BRIAN GREEN

THE GREENS ARE A SOLID young suburban family. They attend church, vote, go to Seahawks' games and Bruce Springsteen concerts. In short, they adhere to typical middle-American standards. Brian is an auto mechanic for high-performance cars and Julie is a nurse. While their eight-year-old boy, Justin, was the initial reason Julie contacted me, the real issue for the couple soon became clear. During the fourteen years they'd been together, things had become routine for both husband and wife. Moreover, they were each growing in different ways, and now yearned for something the other did not provide.

© JANE DE FOREST

SACRED UNION

Sadly, this is a story I often encounter.

Brian wanted more sex. Julie wanted better sex, with intimacy and emotional, spiritual depth.

When I focused my inner intuitive vision, I could "see" Brian's creative-sexual chakra flowing to a computer as if he were being pulled into a vacuum. I saw that online porn had grown like a virus, sucking up his focus and libido and leaving little else for his wife. Julie felt lonely and under-appreciated. With the grind of parenting, her "sexy-self" had taken a back seat to her "mommy-self."

They were in a rut. But when I tuned in intuitively to their "relationship energy", it had a solid foundation. The current

© TARA DE FOREST

rough spell they were going through was actually an opportunity for new expansion. What and how Brian and Julie regarded each other was critical. The choice to move past resentment and forgive each other, I strongly sensed, would elevate the energy of their marriage to a new level of harmony. Then passion and romance could have the best chance to flourish. It was up to them.

My job? To help Julie and Brian remember the feeling they shared of being in love.

When I work with couples, the first step is to help them mentally move from their heads to their hearts. By conjuring up the feeling and emotional connection of the "good old days," the couple begins to remember the foundation of love

© TARA DE FOREST

that has always existed. This can be challenging, so I gave this pair a thirty-day assignment to "spoon" together and breathe simultaneously using a tantric technique.

TANTRIC BREATHING TECHNIQUE

THIS FIVE-THOUSAND-YEAR-OLD HINDU practice is really my secret weapon. It is a shame that tantra is not better understood and sometimes gets a scandalous rap in the U.S., because the breathing technique can bring a couple into harmony within five minutes. This practice emphasizes oneness with each other through "entrainment." In my couple's consultations, I have each pair breathe together in slow regular breaths, which "entrains" the electro-magnetic field of the heart. Then they breathe in the opposite pattern: as one breathes in, the other breathes out, passing the breath back and forth. The next step is to picture a color and shape to the breath. Infusing the breath with positive regard and unconditional love is the last step. Practicing this can be extremely powerful in creating the mental and emotional space to attract Eros. The truth is "falling in love" can't be implemented or forced. Authentic *simpatico* is a thing that grows from a tended garden.

I am delighted to report that Brian and Julie followed through with the exercises, and chose gratitude instead of animosity. Within a few months, the Greens were back in the groove and Julie's crooked smile let me know their passion was rekindled too.

Justin? He is the real winner.

LAUREL AND RICHARD REALLY LOVE each other. Thirty-
something, urban, kind and well educated, with three kids,
they are making their way in the world. They have been
partners for a number of years and are both on their spiritual
path—they have everything going for them. Laurel's fighting
style, however, is to erupt like Mt. Vesuvius from time to time,
and Richard's is "death by a thousand cuts," in near constant
low-grade hostility.

My intuitive core told me there was emotional inflammation in
their relationship energy-basket. That irritation made it hard
to cope successfully with "garden variety" life problems. They
were constantly in a state of agitation.

I also clearly saw that while Laurel and Richard loved each
other deeply, their biggest issue was fear. They each doubted
the other's commitment and true feelings. Often partners don't
realize how much love underlies the patina of an old, corroded
connection.

In our follow-up appointment, I was not prepared to see
the thin, luminescent strands that connected their chakras
(energy centers at intervals along the spine that correlate with
certain organs, colors and qualities). Richard explained that
in addition to using the tantric breathing techniques, they
incorporated Reiki (a form of hands-on energy healing using
focused intention and symbols). I also felt an intense loving

energy between them—they were choosing harmony.

I often "see" relationship energy as a vital, pulsing connection in the form of a container I call a "marriage basket," created energetically each time the couple makes love, and steeped with the feelings they share. Too much negative regard directed at each other will blow a hole in that basket as surely as infidelity will. Sometimes I see a hole in a couple's shared energy that has been patched up, as a result of forgiveness healing their union.

The lack of vital, pulsing connection is often the problem, even when both people share history and love for each other. Passion, emotional intimacy and the feeling of being madly in love that filled the early stages of their relationship with excitement and intrigue are long gone. No wonder over half of the marriages in America end in divorce. Many of our friends who married young have already split, or are living lives of quiet desperation. Why? Is this the death of long-term romantic, fulfilling, deep love? It simply doesn't have to be.

There are many contributing factors in our complex society and busy lifestyles that make sustaining an intimate relationship a challenge. We want considerably more out of our relationships than did prior generations. For the better part of human history, arranged marriages were financial and social contracts between families. By the Middle Ages, marriage began to include love and romance. The current relationship model might incorporate an extensive list of expectations: fun, adventure, great conversation, compassionate listening, common interests, love, romance, security, respect, toned bodies, being best friends . . . AND having great sex!

Yet from my observation, what couples seem to yearn for most is a deeper spiritual-emotional connection . . . a "soul mate." The sex is secondary, often with the understanding that physical intimacy can be enhanced as a natural outcome of a loving union without boundaries.

Psychotherapy and marriage counseling are two wonderful ways to help work through problems, and I may refer a couple if they don't already have help, because I am not a therapist or psychologist. But many an hour can be spent maneuvering for favor with the couple's therapist instead of addressing the fundamental issues. Our minds are extremely clever and when the couple is focused on winning. That focus is a clear sign they are approaching each other from the ego's perspective. So, regardless of how much time or money is spent consulting professionals or family and friends, there is still a game being played within an "ego mindset."

From my intuitive sessions, I've been surprised by how often people's minds and hearts are enticed away from each other while still within a committed relationship. The thrill of an extramarital affair and the temptation of forbidden fruit are more likely to coax either partner into contemplating betrayal if the door of opportunity is opened energetically. This energetic door opens when one of the pair mistakenly focuses on such negative, destructive thought. But when passion and a focused imagination are combined with strong emotion, an energetic power-tool is created that can bring about change quickly. I always encourage a couple to keep their passionate focus within the psychic-emotional boundaries of their partnership.

When the couple re-establishes harmony with their hearts, the rest seems to fall into place. I guide the couple to move awareness from the everyday world to a higher perspective, by teaching them to entrain, breathe, and vision together . . . to fall *back* in love.

In my intuitive practice, I also incorporate the indigenous wisdom I gleaned from my Lakota Medicine Woman teacher. A key visualization in this wisdom tradition is to journey through an altered state of consciousness into your authentic spark-of-God self. Most often referred to as "soul retrieval", the point of the process-journey is to collect the fragmented parts of the person's psyche that were taken or inadvertently left behind during an experience of trauma, argument or abandonment. I also encourage guided meditation with a rhythmic beat, focusing on retrieving fragmented parts of the relationship. I record my "one love" meditation so each couple can listen to it for thirty or so days while they are going to sleep. My approach is a fusion of ancient and indigenous traditions (ones that humans have been practicing for millennia, now residing in our collective DNA) in conjunction with producing my drawings that I intuit for each client.

When people choose to think differently, I can see the resulting transformation in my mind's eye during a reading. When people's perceptions change, so do their attitudes; then ideas and thought patterns shift. This, in turn, alters people's energy fields. The most amazing aspect to me is that I can see the energetic change in real time. It's a game changer when the couple focuses simply on the positive in each other. It seems that honoring your beloved from a higher perspective can be a relatively painless first step toward a more peaceful and harmonious union. I am optimistic that Eros, the god of love, has merely suffered a near-death experience. Thankfully, now resuscitated, he will open the door for a new renaissance in the committed relationship.

Out beyond ideas of wrongdoing and right doing,
There is a field.
I'll meet you there.

RUMI - 13TH CENTURY

CHAPTER 9

SHE TOOK
THE TRAIN
TO HEAVEN

© TARA DE FOREST

SHE TOOK THE TRAIN TO HEAVEN

The names and location in this story have been changed.

*Art must be an expression of love
or it is nothing.*

MARC CHAGALL

POWERFUL PRE-DEATH DREAMS THAT come in the last days and moments before transitioning to the other side can be important guidance for the dying person. These visionary end-of-life dreams in ancient civilizations were regarded as religious experiences. It was a common event in the pre-modern world for an angel, relative or guardian to assist the soul in navigating its way through to the afterlife. In cultural traditions around the world, pre-death dreams are spiritually significant, and in indigenous cultures, they are considered real visitations from the ancestors or from Great Spirit. It is expected that a shaman will interpret the visions of the dying in order to provide guidance for the journey to the afterlife.

> *"People in present day society experience pre-death dreams with remarkable frequency, although in many cases people today do not know what to make of such strange, visionary experiences. Living as we do in the culture where scientific authorities*

© JANE DE FOREST

SHE TOOK THE TRAIN
TO HEAVEN

assure us that dreaming is nothing more than
a random firing of neurons in the brain, people
who happen to experience an incredibly powerful
pre-death dream often question their own sanity
and mental health. (But) as a direct result of the
dream or vision there arises a new understanding
of living, dying and that which lies beyond death."

DREAMING BEYOND DEATH:
A GUIDE TO PRE-DEATH DREAMS AND VISIONS
by Kelly Bulkeley and Rev. Patricia Bulkley

"I'm not afraid to die, Janie," said Beth, as she peered calmly into my face.

"I had a dream last night. It was so real. My father came to me. He was standing on a platform by a train. The door was open and I could feel the excitement of departure in the air as the steamy smoke curled upward. He said, 'Bethie, go buy a ticket because the train is leaving the station.' It felt like he was really there," Beth said, obviously moved by the dream.

We both had a hunch this was no ordinary dream; it appeared to be a classic pre-death visitation.

Her father, Bernie, had died only a few years before, and Beth had cared for him until the very end. Her mother had succumbed to cancer when Beth was a teenager, and that death had been an earthquake within her family of seven.

"It really feels like your father's soul has come to help you find your way back home," I said.

Beth smiled weakly. The breast cancer had rendered her once-strong runner's body frail, unable to do much more than sit up, much less walk.

Beth leaned heavily into me as I steadied her feeble steps from the sofa and down the hall to her bedroom. I pulled the covers up and they enveloped her. Kneeling on the floor, I gazed into her sky-blue eyes, and was grateful that we all survive death.

With my developed sixth sense, I have gathered quite a lot of unusual descriptions of what heaven, our real home, is like, from souls who have passed over to the other side of life. I've gleaned there is a "place" or dimension that we return to after life—a place surrounded by our loved ones and imbued with an over-whelming peace. We never die alone. There is always a guardian, ancestor, angel, Jesus or Buddha, or guiding light to help us find our way. We are met with unconditional love and acceptance. I have not encountered a judging God to punish us for our earthly sins, although I often recognize karmic repercussions for our actions while in "Earth school." But I'm not someone who knows the whole story — I am merely reporting the wisdom I have gleaned from many encounters with the other side.

Beth and I gazed at each other and the room melted away. We both loved each other like sisters. She was a confidante, and my best friend. I realized there would be a gaping hole in my life when she passed away, and I could feel panic in the pit of my stomach.

Jane, this isn't about you! I chided myself. Of course she will survive death and her real self will return Home to heaven. But I selfishly wanted her to stay. The anger that rose in my heart seemed to push the panic out.

Nevertheless, I admit the possibility of cancer had crossed my mind. Although Beth had generally lived a healthy life, eating organic food and exercising daily, she had allowed a seed of anger to take root in her heart. She fed the seed with regular negative thoughts and strong emotions. It seemed to grow into a tree that bore bitter fruit. Beth's oncologist was direct: the only option was chemotherapy and radiation.

When I told Beth about some research on turkey-tail mushrooms in clinical studies for breast cancer patients, she was captivated. The common polypore had reportedly helped build the body's immune system and had been used in conjunction with chemotherapy. I have found three or four medicinal mushrooms with reported anti-cancer and anti-tumor qualities. We both knew it was too late, but what we did have was that moment together.

"Bring your awareness to your breath," I continued. "Good.

"Follow your breath in, filling your belly . . . let your breath out. Just be aware of your breath, the rise and fall of your chest.

"Observe your thoughts as if they are white puffy clouds gently moving across a clear blue sky. Watch them float by and try not to think those thoughts . . . let them go. Don't go inside of the thought, just bring your awareness to it.

"Name the thought. 'Pain thought.'"

"Wondering thought," whispered Beth. "Sad thought. Daydream."

"Don't judge yourself for any thought, just be aware of it and observe it." I trailed off.

A detailed train station scene with a clear storyline blossomed in my imagination, as I used my sixth sense. Colors, feelings, ambiance and an undeniable urgency . . . there was not much time left.

Then slam! I was there in the train station, feeling the brisk air, the smell of diesel fuel, and the excitement of a new adventure.

My gut was telling me I could guide her with imagery and meditation that might help her find her way back home to heaven.

The journey Home seems to be a shared human experience, and many ancient cultures have an established guide to help the departed find their way back to their ancestors. In ancient Egypt, *The Egyptian Book of the Dead* was Egyptians' primary guide for the soul to traverse the complicated afterlife. Similarly, *The Tibetan Book of The Dead* has been used in that mountainous country to guide souls after death through levels of consciousness called the *bardo*.

I imagined Beth and me, encircled by golden light, filled with love and compassion. Then I anchored my life-force energy in the earth like a giant tree root, strong and vital. I drew up life-force energy with my breath and imagined the earth flowing upwards through my spine. Simultaneously, I saw a sparkling fresh green light with energy filling my body, clearing my energy, and pushing "what I no longer need to carry" out the top of my head.

"Can you picture that train station," I asked softly, "where your smiling father is standing on the platform at the waiting train? Just like the dream, but now it is real. With an open heart, your father welcomes you. There is a smell of diesel fuel and creosote, rusted tracks, and a shiny silver train that reflects the azure blue sky.

"Your father gestures to you to get your ticket. There's a big smile on his face. Now see yourself going inside the station, smell the old wood, and feel the deep green marble counter that's cool to your touch. 'OPEN' is painted in gold letters, and a gentle woman with kind eyes and strong hands gives you a ticket."

I caught my breath. The sweetness of the moment hit me.
Beth was resting peacefully with a smile on her face. Sunlight
streamed into the cluttered bedroom filled with framed photos
from happier times, books, indigenous art, her art . . . and
bottles and bottles of medicine.

Outside, a flowering plum relinquished its pink petals to the
breeze and cascaded like confetti at a charmed wedding. The
rain stopped; water and air mixed, forming a halo around
the lighted parts of things. I could see Mt. St. Helen's purple
shadows gracing her white peaks.

I was grateful to be sharing this moment with one of my
dearest friends in this life. All we really have is this moment.
The present moment is ever changing, never the same. All
things are always in motion, being created, then destroyed,
rising, then falling away.

I remembered the lessons of my Buddhist teachers, seemingly
elusive and mysterious. I could never quite grasp them,

although I could quote them verbatim. I had understood them only as intellectual concepts with foreign-sounding names.

Yet in the unlikely clutter of Beth's bedroom where I knelt, the moment opened up. It extended slowly, expanding exponentially, until it incorporated everything—like an intelligent matrix of which I was an integral part. I thought, *Is this the web of life? Are we really part of a unity of everything, like a system?*

A living matrix?

Yet there was no more "me" to think the thought. Just "nothing." Oh, and "everything" too. For a fleeting moment, I experienced something huge. Maybe it was the Eternal Now.

Beth fidgeted. I returned to my guided meditation with a lingering feeling of infinity.

"As you greet your father and find your seat on the train, it jolts and pulls out from the station.

"You are off.

"Faster, faster, rolling hills and countryside pass outside the window.

"Faster—the view is blurring as you pick up speed.

"Everything is going to be okay.

"Everything is perfect. You are going home.

"The train car doors open onto a platform. It's summertime. Puffy clouds dot a mauve and peach sky. Warm sunlight sparkles on a flowing waterfall surrounded by hanging flower baskets and rose gardens. Emerald grass is framed by flowerbeds, and you see people you love who have passed over: your mother, your grandparents, your friends, aunts and uncles.

© JANE DE FOREST

They are all smiling, welcoming you home and sending you love, compassion, goodness. They love you so much and are overjoyed to see you. Everyone is alive and well. Unconditional love and acceptance permeate the air," I said, in a soft voice.

Beth was now calm, a rarity with all her pain and anxiety.

My eyes closed, too, and I could see a tree-lined park filled with people. Beth and her father were standing on the platform, being greeted by their loved ones and animals. I felt joyful, calm, accepted. Tears ran down my cheeks as if I were at that train station with her.

"You are home now. The train will be waiting for you at the station when you are ready and you will return to this place where there is peace and all your loved ones. Remember this journey Beth, remember when it is time to go . . . this is the way home," I said.

The room was quiet. I knew we had created sacred space. The air was thick with a powerful presence. The transition from this life, through death, to the next life is a holy and reverent sacred journey from the physical world to a higher plane of existence.

My next visit was one of the last during which Beth was lucid and still herself. We talked about dying and going home. I suggested that we consider establishing a sign she could send to let me know she had arrived safe and sound.

I explained to Beth, "My grandmother and I agreed she would let me know when she made it home and everything was all right. The sign my grandmother chose was a butterfly. My sixth sense told me she was communicating with me soon after death when I saw a hundred tiny butterflies fluttering in the warm sun. It was a July day by an alpine lake and an electromagnetic shock tingled up my spine, making me shudder. I had just been reflecting on her journey Home at that moment and I guess my grandmother didn't want me to miss the message that she had made it to her heavenly destination. The event was especially significant because she had been a devout atheist, but for some inexplicable reason, in her last days, she began to entertain the possibility that there might be more than the material, rational world.

Maybe because in the end, her father began to appear in the hospital. Floating on the ceiling, wearing the long white sleeping gown and cap he wore in life at the turn of the century. No one could see or hear him but his daughter—my grandmother. She enjoyed their conversations and told me matter-of-factly that he had come to take her Home when the time was right.

"Do you like the idea of a sign?" I asked hopefully.

" I love that idea," answered Beth. "A hummingbird would be a perfect sign."

"What kind?" I asked playfully. Beth liked the idea of sending messages through signs; it made sense to her. Her artwork was filled with symbolism—the language of the soul and Mother Nature, both concepts she loved.

"The kind of hummingbird with an iridescent green-blue breast. That will be my sign."

HUMMINGBIRD: THIS SPIRIT-ANIMAL SYMBOLIZES ENDURANCE, COURAGE AND FEARLESSNESS. THEIR LONG JOURNEY, SOMETIMES OVER HUNDREDS OF MILES OF WATER AND LAND, REQUIRES TRUST AND COURAGE. A 3,000-MILE TRIP EACH WAY THAT THE HUMMINGBIRD TRAVELS FROM NORTH AMERICA (ALASKA INCLUDED) TO CENTRAL AMERICA IS TRULY REMARKABLE. THEY WILL OFTEN RETURN TO THE VERY SAME GARDEN YEAR AFTER YEAR. A HUMBLE BIRD IN STATURE, THE HUMMINGBIRD REACHES HER DISTANT DESTINATION USING HER TREMENDOUS STRENGTH. BUT THIS ANIMAL-MESSENGER ALSO COMMUNICATES JOY, LIGHTNESS OF BEING, AND RESILIENCY. IT CAN FLY BACKWARDS, SIDE TO SIDE AND STOP IN MID-FLIGHT, CERTAINLY REMARKABLE FOR A WINGED ONE. IN FLIGHT, HER WINGS MAKE A FIGURE EIGHT . . . OR MAYBE IT'S AN INFINITY SYMBOL.

The "Journey Home Meditation" was a weekly train trip that Beth and I took. As her life force drained and she came closer to death, we took the journey every other day. Even though by the end, she was comatose, that did not stop me from going through our guided meditation, since the subconscious hears everything. Her bald head was beautiful in a strange way, and I was grateful her suffering was almost over. She became unable to communicate with me, and one lovely summer morning she died. Leaving her old cancer-ridden costume on the bed, she journeyed home to heaven.

"Jane, look at this." Her partner of twenty years pressed a

notecard into my hand with an astonished expression on his face. On the first sympathy card was a beautifully painted garden. My heart raced. In the foreground was an artistic hummingbird, and yes, it had a blue-green breast.

She had made it home! I was sure—well, pretty sure. Had this serendipity materialized for someone else's best friend, it would have been obvious to me, and I would have said, "Yes, of course it is an after-death communication. Clearly." But because it was my serendipity, a small part of me doubted.

The last rays of the setting sun raked across my deck as I watched the warm light bathe the purple wisteria. I felt calm. The memorial was over, Beth was gone. But there was a hole in my heart. Then I heard buzzing . . . humming.

Two hummingbirds appeared and hovered in front of me. They peered into my face. My body involuntarily shuddered as I took in the surreal scene. The hum of their tiny wings filled my brain as the birds stayed exactly in place, as if resting on air. Messengers? They stayed for a long time, watching me. It felt like a dream. I could not accurately measure the time because the moment seemed beyond time and space.

But my heart was full, and my whole body felt tingly on the surface. Beth was sending a message. I was sure she had made it home. There was no doubt in my mind. My guess? She traveled by train.

If the dream is a translation of waking life,
waking life is also a translation of the dream.
RENE MAGRITTE

CHAPTER 10

GETTING
FREE

© TARA DE FOREST

Getting Free: New Information Can Help You Shift Gears

A human being is a part of the whole, called by us "universe", a part limited in time and space. He experiences himself, his thoughts and feelings as something separated from the rest, a kind of optical delusion of his consciousness. This delusion is a kind of prison for us, restricting us to our personal desires and to affection for a few persons nearest to us. Our task must be to free ourselves from this prison by widening our circle of compassion to embrace all living creatures and the whole of nature in its beauty.

ALBERT EINSTEIN

THE UNEXPECTED

TOM HAD DIED FOUR YEARS earlier and his entire family—his mother, father, wife and sister, Ara—were assembled in their Washington home. We settled into their cozy living room for my intuitive consultation. I "read" and reported specific details that there was no way I could have known with my conscious mind, details that indicated Tom was present to his family members. Ironically, the piece of information that convinced the family I was the "real McCoy" was so outlandish I almost didn't mention it.

During the sober and reverent spirit communication session, a powerful feeling came from the other end of the living room.

Centering, I sensed movement and got the impression of dancing. I wondered if Tom was trying to communicate a romantic evening his wife and he had shared, possibly arm in arm at their wedding. Instead, I could vaguely make out the transparent silhouette of a portly man doing . . . the waltz, no . . . the moon walk? NO, the chicken dance! I did a doubletake. *Really?* I thought. I re-centered. Certainly this was a misread, yet there again I watched the unmistakable arm motion on the now more opaque energy of Tom. *I can't possibly tell his grieving family this!* Once I broke through my concern about upsetting the family if I was wrong, I mumbled, "I think maybe . . . well . . . say . . . what do you think about the chicken dance?"

The entire family burst into laughter, startling the elderly father awake in his easy chair. Tom apparently loved to, yes, you guessed it, do the chicken dance. This established my credibility, which was important to Ara, as the next piece of information changed her life.

Ara and Tom had a running joke that she would take her brother's middle name when he passed because Ara was without one. When he died, Ara legally did just that, but was consumed with guilt and paralyzed with fear. Ara was terrified she had offended and angered her brother on the other side.

In my mind's eye I saw Tom bent down on one knee, kissing his sister's hand. The gesture was a heartfelt acknowledgement and was a clear communication of Tom's overwhelming love. I conveyed all this to her to the best of my ability, as well as the

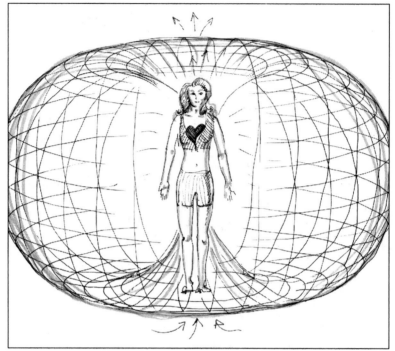

© JANE DE FOREST

HUMAN ELECTROMAGNETIC FIELD GENERATED BY THE HEART

his profound love and concern for peace with his sister. She wept. In a heartbeat she let go of a good bit of the guilt and fear that had burdened her for years.

Eyes closed, I watched with my sixth sense, as the dark cloud around her abdomen dissipated, and her energy lightened and expanded like a flower opening in time-lapse photography. As she changed her perception about the situation, her reality changed in real time.

Soon after that session she packed her belongings and moved from where she'd isolated herself in another state, changing location in order to be near her family. She got a new job, and the last I heard she was living a vital and happy life.

This is the power of receiving information that is beyond that of our our rational mind, information that speaks to the heart, and ultimately can assist in personal growth. We all have thoughts gumming up the works, but new information can help us shift gears.

WHO ARE WE, I MEAN REALLY?

TERMS SUCH AS THE "deeper self", the "intuitive core" or the "higher nature" all describe the internal "Siri" guidance system that resides within you. I think of our innate intuitive system as pre-consciousness and pre-verbal. Accessing this *knowing* that is already inside you empowers you, deepens the quality of your *chi* and increases your electro-magnetic field, among other things.

"Charisma" and "animal magnetism" are words we use to describe the almost tangible feeling of someone who possesses strong personal power. This energetic aspect of yourself is invisible, intangible and unquantifiable—it is your eternal-self, that part of you that never dies. There is a part of you that is ageless and beyond time. THIS is the part of you we are seeking to help emerge and then incorporate into your conscious self, through training.

Throughout history, many saints and holy beings are said to

have had a strong loving aura, accompanied by a physical light. Sometimes called a halo, this idea can be seen clearly in literature (the Bible) and art. I believe we are looking at the same energy but calling "whatever-it-is" by different names. How the label is applied depends on whether it is being described by a scientist or an aborigine, atheist or fundamentalist, child, or elder nearing death. Regardless, the "whatever-it-is" has been recognized in most cultures and societies throughout history as an energetic, circulating, animating, living force within every human and every living thing, too.

LIFE-FORCE ENERGY

氣, IS THE CHINESE CHARACTER for the "life-force energy", which is also known as ch'i or chi. The ancient Chinese tradition of medicine and philosophy is based on the foundation of the existence and management of chi— the life-force energy. Grace and Holy Spirit in Christianity; *qi*, and ch'i in China; chi in Igbo people of Nigeria; *ki* in Japan; *ka* in ancient Egypt; *khi* in Vietnam; *gi* in Korea; *prana* in India; *mana* in Polynesian; *ha* in Hawaiian Huna; *wakan* in Lakota Sioux; *maban* in Australian aboriginal; *awen* in Welsh; *baraka* in Islamic; *rLung* in Tibetian; dark energy in physics, or "The Force" a la Star Wars.

WHAT MOST PEOPLE WANT
AND WHY THEY DON'T GET IT

REALLY, WHAT MOST PEOPLE WANT is a generally harmonious, prosperous, and healthy life, one where they do meaningful work and are surrounded by genuine and loving people. Sure, we would all like a little more money, but at the top of the list what most crave is belonging, having heartfelt connections and doing meaningful work. The spiritual masters tell us to follow our hearts, but that can be elusive: anger, disappointment, and resentment can take up big spaces in our hearts. The problem is, negative thoughts beget negative moods and dark energy that cause our emotions to spiral downward. But the reverse is also true: a positive, grateful attitude creates a warm, safe and welcoming terrain that people are drawn to and where good things grow.

Changing your own reality is the first step in using your free will and changing the effect you have on others and on the world. Because these moods, light or dark, have a much greater effect on the world around us than we could ever imagine. In intuitive consultations, I have witnessed time and time again that when people shift their thinking, they shift their reality in that moment. The process is nothing less than miraculous and is the most empowering aspect of the work I do.

People sometimes come in for a reading and give themselves away—and I mean exactly that. On occasion I've had to tell clients not to give me their power. I am not a fortuneteller or a therapist—all I can offer is a higher, or at least different, perspective. We are ultimately responsible for our own actions and that is what I see as an intuitive. We all have an effect on the world in what we say, and most potent of all, what we think. I like to help people foster strength and self-reliance because there is then a better chance of helping them get to a place of connection and creativity.

WE DON'T DIE

MY CLIENTS HAVE GIVEN ME the priceless gift of helping me become a more spiritual person. I am humbled by the wisdom that people and animals, on both this and the other side of the veil, have given me. Through those who are living who have asked me to connect with those who have passed, I have developed a vague understanding of the afterlife and have come to think there is a higher spiritual authority that transcends specific religions or ideology. I see this higher spiritual authority—or God or Creator—as intelligent, compassionate, light, not because I want to, but because that is what I have seen. I've come to understand there is an order or pattern within the universe, a matrix. Maybe that's what God is—a loving, intelligent matrix.

I see us as part of a whole creation that looks like a web of light; there is no way you could ever be on the outside looking in, because by the nature of being alive, you are connected to everything. I have also come to understand there is nothing to fear in death because, well . . . we don't die!

A fascinating dimension of an intuitive consultation is that — regardless of whether someone is deeply religious or a non-believer— with my sixth sense, I can see an aspect of the person that seems ageless or eternal. When a person's relatives from the other side make an appearance, they are very much alive. It is hard for me to think of them as dead when they are animated in front of me, having a conversation, or rather, a "communication." It is my contention that I could not be having a conversation about current events with a person who would have had no knowledge of these events while they were "alive" if the person or animal were truly dead.

WHAT THEY HAVE TO SAY

OFTEN DURING A COMMUNICATION WITH a person or animal on the other side, the conversation includes specific information. My favorite experience is drawing accurate layouts and elevations of buildings and rooms, such as where the furniture is placed, and sometimes even color schemes. I receive images in my imagination that can include physical features, and exact words or phrases that were significant while that person was alive. An example can be found in chapter three where the phrase "I Love You To The Moon And Back" was important to the family of the woman who had passed away.

WE COME BACK

WHEN I FIRST STARTED DOING this work, I did not believe in past lives. But what I have "seen" is that people's souls, or perhaps one might call them spirits or light, return to this world to spend other lifetimes on planet Earth in the guise of human beings. The best analogy I have is a "hand in glove", viz., the soul or light is the hand, and the physical body is the glove. We go hand in glove, if you will, and the glove seems to be different in each lifetime. As we transition through various lifetimes, we experience bodies that are different in race, gender, and socioeconomic status.

What is touching and hopeful, moreover, is that we tend to return in spiritual family groups. I get the impression that we reincarnate in clusters, taking turns being the mother, father, daughter, son, best friend, neighbor, etc. Instant chemistry and the feeling of knowing someone without ever having met them before is a common occurrence with many people. Conversely, there are certainly times people feel an inexplicable disdain for someone others might consider a perfectly nice person. People can also have instant rapport with another culture or time period. For example, a young college student I read for recently loved old Louie Armstrong-type jazz. He not only could play this style easily on several instruments, his musical

© TARA de FOREST

A PAST LIFE
IN EARTH SCHOOL

compositions reflected that era. Often my clients report a sense of "déjà vu" with people, places, and foreign cultures. I suspect these are indications of some sort of past-life memory.

SIXTH SENSE

THE TRUTH IS, AS SPECIAL as my intuitive skills make me appear, they are not unique. We ALL have a rich and broad spectrum of sixth-sense ability. All animals, human animals included, have an intuitive "Siri" system for survival and evolution. "Second sight" as it is sometime called, is an internal guidance system. It is in this way, you, yes you, have access to information beyond your rational thoughts and learned ideas. Second sight is also the tool I teach for sending and receiving telepathic information in my class, "I Knew You Were Going To Say That."

Our ancestors used their developed sixth sense to locate hunting grounds, meet up with tribal members, and predict when an enemy tribe might attack. Black Elk had a vision, or what we might call a realistic dream, of his tribal land being overrun with iron ribbons and the death of his people and their native ways. As we know all too well, the prophecy came true, showing the information was accurate.

Our sixth sense has a broad spectrum of intuitive ability. Most people are adept at one or two of these forms of information. Imagine that your intuitive spectrum is a rainbow, in which only a narrow area, say yellow and blue, is developed. That might equate to strength in interpreting gut feelings and getting future flashes. But as more of your intuitive spectrum is developed, a greater variety of authentic and USABLE information is available to you.

Aspects of intuition and some ways this kind of knowledge manifests are:

1. Knowing someone you've never met before

2. Knowing someone's thoughts, feelings, or intentions (gut feeling)

3. Knowing what someone is going to say before they say it (pre-knowledge)

4. Knowing what is about to happen (pre-cognitive thought)

5. Knowing you have been in the same circumstances before *(déjà vu)*

6. Knowing what is happening elsewhere (for example, mothers sensing their child is in danger or having "eyes in the back" of the mother's head)

7. Knowing when someone is lying

8. Knowing a concept or idea in its entirety, such as an invention or creation

9. Knowing the symbolic meaning of information within synchronicities or patterns in seemingly random coincidences

PSYCHIC DEVELOPMENT AND
ACCESSING YOUR NATURAL INTUITION

RECEIVING TELEPATHIC MESSAGES (knowing information without being told), being precognitive (knowing about a potential future event) and obtaining non-local information (knowledge about something that's somewhere else or someone who's somewhere else) is quite simple to do with practice. I use a several-hundred-year-old method of drawing the received information in pictures and symbols.

Sometimes called "remote viewing", this technique of observing and documenting information from a distant location is popular. It is by far the easiest way to get past one's rational mind to access accurate telepathic information that comes from a pre-verbal place in the psyche. Remote viewing is a technique that was developed at the Stanford Research Institute, where investigations were conducted into the human mind's capacity for expanded awareness. In this kind of awareness, people are able to envision distant places and future events with only geographic coordinates. I use the technique because it is a clean way to open my mind and broaden my perspective.

I trained myself to "read" a person "cold" with no foreknowl- edge, images or personal information. It is the most difficult type of intuitive reading. I learned the language of my core was symbolic, and from there I cultivated additional areas of my intuitive range, or spectrum. A several-hundred-year-old method of drawing the received information in pictures and symbols, makes getting clear information easier. The language of the psychic core is symbolism, so it is more efficient to sketch than explain it with words. I often render exact portraits of people I've never met before. In my intuitive training workshops I teach seven primary modes of your sixth- sense spectrum, but there are a few more that are extremely subtle. With practice, you can become quite accurate, but it takes a bit of time to train your internal guidance system.

I WILL SOON TEACH YOU MY SECRETS

FOR FURTHER STUDY, my self-directed program and workbook or playbook will be coming out soon. The exercises will utilize a form of artwork sometimes called mandala, or balanced images contained within a circle. I have created a program to begin to master the *power of you*. It's not necessary that you practice everyday, but the more consistent you are, the more successfully you'll awaken to your authentic, beautiful self and welcome a life with more meaning, purpose and joy become.

You can program your internal Siri guidance system with pictures and, with practice, you can become quite accurate, it takes a bit of time to train your internal guidance system. More to come.

© TARA DE FOREST

THE MOST IMPORTANT FRONTIER

Dear Reader,

Please Keep In Touch
If you would like to send me feedback or stories
of your own, I would love to hear from you.
janesinspiration@gmail.com

If you liked this book . . . and would like to
share this information with others, please
consider writing an Amazon review! **www.**
amazon.com

To Book A Sesson, intuitive consulation,
coaching, or workshop, please contact
www.janesinspiration.com

To Purchase Prints of Illustrations, please visit
www.janesinspiration.com

SHOUT OUT

Publishing coach & launch expert, Linda Stirling
linda@thepublishingcircle.com

Business coach, Mindy Cockrell
palettefullofsunshine@gmail.com

Human Design / Personal & Professional Development
Ruth Brennan
ruth@embraceflux.com

Sacred Site Travel, Jerry Miner
jerryminer730@gmail.com

BIBLIOGRAPHY

© TARA de FOREST

BIBLIOGRAPHY

Alexander, E. (2014) *The Map of Heaven: How Science, Religion, and Ordinary People are Proving the Afterlife.* New York, NY, United States: Simon & Schuster.

Alexander, E. and Alex, E. (2012) *Proof of Heaven: A Neurosurgeon's Journey into the Afterlife.* New York, NY: Simon & Schuster Paperbacks.

Bohm, D. (2002) *Wholeness and the Implicate Order.* New York: Taylor & Francis.

Bowman, C. (1997) *Children's Past Lives: How Past Life Memories Affect Your Child.* New York: Bantam Dell Pub Group (Trd).

Braden, G. (2006) *The Divine Matrix: Bridging Time, Space, Miracles, and Belief.* Carlsbad, CA: Hay House.

Brennan, B.A. and Smith, J.A. (1990) *Hands of Light: A Guide to Healing Through the Human Energy Field: A New Paradigm for the Human Being in Health, Relationship, and Disease* (Bantam New Age Books). New York: Bantam Books (Transworld Publishers, a division of the Random House Group).

Bukowski, C. and Martin, J. (2009) *The People Look Like Flowers at Last, New Poems.* New York: HarperCollins eBooks.

Bulkeley, Bulkley, P., Bulkeley, P.K. and Bulkeley, K. (2005) *Dreaming Beyond Death: A Guide to Pre-Death Dreams and Visions.* Boston, MA: Beacon Press.

Cameron, J. (1997) *The Artist's Way: A Spiritual Path to Higher Creativity.* London: Pan Books.

Campbell, J. (2012) *The Hero with a Thousand Faces.* 3rd edn. United States: New World Library.

Campbell, J. and Moyers, B.D. (1988) *The Power of Myth.* New York, NY: Doubleday Books.

Choquette, S. and CHOQUETTE (1995) *The Psychic Pathway: A Workbook for Reawakening the Voice of Your Soul.* New York: Carol Trade Paperbacks.

Cooper, J.C. and Archer, G.E. (1982) *Symbolism, the Universal Language.* 3rd edn. London, United Kingdom: Aquarian Press.

Cottrell, D.J.M. (2004) *Secrets of Life: Unique Insight into the Workings of Your Soul by the Most Powerful intuitive of Our Time.* London, Ont.: Many Mansions Press.

von Daniken, E., Heron, M. and Erich von Daniken M. Heron (1990) *Chariots of the Gods? Unsolved Mysteries of the Past.* London: Souvenir Press.

Dass, R. and Dass, R. (1971) *Be Here Now.* New York: Distributed by Crown Pub.

Dispenza, J. (2012) *Breaking the hHabit of Being Yourself: How to Lose Your Mind and Create a New One.* London: Hay House UK.

Dispenza, J. (2014) *You Are the Placebo: Making Your Mind Matter.* London, United Kingdom: Hay House UK.

Edwards, B. (2001) *The New Drawing on the Right Side of the Brain.* London: HarperCollins Publishers.

Freke, T. and Gandy, P. (1997) *The Complete Guide to World Mysticism.* London: Piatkus Books.

Gawain, S. (2002) *Creative Visualization: Use the Power of Your Imagination to Create What You Want in Your Life.* 25th edn. San Rafael, CA: Nataraj Pub./New World Library.

Goodall, J., van Lawick, H. and Wrangham, R. (2009) *In the Shadow of Man.* Boston: Houghton Mifflin Harcourt.

Grof, S. (1985) *Beyond the Brain: Birth, Death, and Transcendence in Psychotherapy.* Albany: State University of New York Press.

Grof, S. (1988) *The Adventure of Self-Discovery: Dimensions of Consciousness and New Perspectives in Psychotherapy and Inner Exploration.* Albany: State University of New York Press.

Grout, P. (2013) *E-squared: Nine Do-It-Yourself Energy Experiments That Prove Your Thoughts Create Your Reality.* 2nd edn. Carlsbad, CA: Hay House Insights.

Hancock, G. (2006) *Supernatural: Meetings with the Ancient Teachers of Mankind.* London: Arrow Books, London.

Hancock, G. and Faiia, S. (1996) *Fingerprints of the Gods: The Evidence of Earth's Lost Civilization.* New York: Crown Publishing Group.

Hawk Spirit Animal (2012) Available at: http://www.spiritanimal.info/hawk-spirit-animal/ (Accessed: 30 November 2016).

Hay, L.L. (1985) You Can Heal Your Life. 2nd edn. Carson, CA: Hay House.

Houston, J. (1982) *The Possible Human: A Course in Extending Your Physical, Mental, and Creative Abilities.* Los Angeles: Jeremy P Tarcher.

Huxley, A. (1977) *The Doors of Perception and Heaven and Hell.* London, United Kingdom: HarperCollins (UK).

Johari, H. (1987) *Tools for Tantra*. Rochester, VT: Inner Traditions: Bear & Company.

Judith, A. (1987) *Wheels of Life: A User's Guide to the Chakra System*. United States: Llewellyn Publications, U.S.

Jung, C.G. and Jung, C. (1997) *Man and His Symbols*. New York: Bantam Doubleday Dell Publishing Group.

Karagulla, S. (1991a) *Breakthrough to Creativity: Your Higher Sense Perception*. 8th edn. Santa Monica, CA: DeVorss & Co ,U.S.

Karagulla, S. (1991b) *Breakthrough to Creativity: Your Higher Sense Perception*. 8th edn. Santa Monica, CA: DeVorss & Co, U.S.

Karagulla, S., van Gelder Kunz, D. and Shafica, K. (1989) *The Chakras and the Human Energy Fields: Correlations Between Medical Science and Clairvoyant Observation*. Wheaton, Ill., U.S.A.: Theosophical Pub. House.

Kübler-Ross, E., Myss, C. and Kubler-Ross, E. (2008) *On Life after Death*. Berkeley, CA: Ten Speed Press.

Lipton, B.H. (2016) *The Biology of Belief 10th Anniversary Edition: Unleashing the Power of Consciousness, Matter & Miracles*. United States: Hay House.

Lipton, B.H. and Bhaerman, S. (2009) *Spontaneous Evolution: Our Positive Future (and a Way to Get There from Here)*. Carlsbad, CA: Hay House.

Masaru, E., Thayne, D.A. and Emoto, M. (2005) *The Hidden Messages in Water*. New York: Simon & Schuster Adult Publishing Group.

McCormick, C. and Grey, A. (1990) *The Sacred Mirrors: The Visionary Art of Alex Grey*. Edited by Ken Wilber. Rochester, VT: Inner Traditions, Bear and Company.

Mcelroy, S.D. (2003) *Animals as Teachers and Healers*. Peter Smith Pub.

McMoneagle, J. (2000) *Remote Viewing Secrets: The Handbook for Developing and Extending Your Psychic Abilities*. New York, NY, United States: Hampton Roads Publishing Company.

McTaggart, L. (2008) *The Intention Experiment: Using Your Thoughts to Change Your Life and the World*. New York: Simon & Schuster Adult Publishing Group.

Monroe, R.A. (1989) *Journeys out of the Body*. London: Souvenir Press.

Moody, R. (2015) *Life after Life: The Bestselling Original Investigation That Revealed 'Near-Death Experiences.'* New York, NY, United States: HarperOne.

Moody, R.A. and Perry, P. (1993) *Reunions: Visionary Encounters with Departed Loved Ones.* New York: Villard Books.

Moody, R. and Perry, P. (2011) *Glimpses of Eternity: Sharing a Loved One's Passage from This Life to the Next.* New York, NY: Ideals Publishing Corporation, U.S.

Morehouse, D.A. (2005) *Remote Viewing: The Complete User's Manual for Coordinate Remote Viewing.* Boulder, CO: Sounds True.

Myss, C., Myss, C. and Shealy, N. (1997) *Anatomy of the Spirit: The Seven Stages of Power and Healing.* New York: Crown Publishing Group.

Newton, M. (1994) *Journey of Souls: Case Studies of Life Between Lives.* Stamford, CT, United States: Llewellyn Publications, U.S.

Newton, M. (2000) *Destiny of Souls: New Case Studies of Life Between Lives.* Stamford, CT, United States: Llewellyn Publications, U.S.

Newton, M. and Institute, the M.N. (2009) *Memories of the Afterlife: Life Between Lives Stories of Personal Transformation.* Woodbury, MN: Llewellyn Publications, U.S.

Peirce, P. (2009) *Frequency: The Power of Personal Vibration.* Hillsboro, Or: Simon & Schuster Adult Publishing Group.

Posted (2012) *Ring! Your Intuition Is Calling.* Available at: http://brainworldmagazine.com/ring-your-intuition-is-calling/ (Accessed: 30 November 2016).

Power Animals *** (2016) Available at: https://www.warpath-s2peacepipes.com/native-american-culture/power-animals.htm (Accessed: 30 November 2016).

Radin, D. (2009) *Entangled Minds: Extrasensory Experiences in a Quantum Reality.* United States: Pocket Books.

Radin, D. (2013) *Supernormal: Science, Yoga, and the Evidence for Extraordinary Psychic Abilities.* New York, NY, United States: Crown Publishing Group.

Schulz, M.L. and Northrup, C. (1998) *Awakening Intuition: Using Your Mind-Body Network for Insight and Healing.* New York: Crown Publications.

Sheldrake, R. (2013) *The Sense of Being Stared at: And Other Unexplained Powers of Human Minds.* New York, NY, United States: Inner Traditions International.

Sheldrake, R., McKenna, T., Abraham, R. and Houston, J. (2001) *Chaos, Creativity, and Cosmic Consciousness.* Rochester, VT: Inner Traditions Bear & Company.

Smith, H. (1993) *Forgotten Truth: The Common Vision of the World's Religions.* San Francisco: HarperCollins Publishers.

Sugrue, T. (1977) *There Is a River: The Story of Edgar Cayce.* S.l.: Dell Pub Co.

Swann, I. and Allen, P.G. (1999) *Psychic Sexuality: The Bio-Psychic 'Anatomy' of Sexual Energies.* Rapid City, SD: Ingo Swann Books.

Swann, I., Swann and Ferguson, M. (1991) *Everybody's Guide to Natural ESP: Unlocking the Extrasensory Power of Your Mind.* Los Angeles: J.P. Tarcher.

Talbot, M. and McTaggart, L. (2011) The Holographic Universe: *The Revolutionary Theory of Reality.* New York, NY: HarperCollins Publishers.

Targ, R. and Houston, J. (2004) *Limitless Mind: A Guide to Remote Viewing and Transformation of Consciousness.* Malden, MA, United States: New World Library.

Targ, R. and Schwartz, S.A. (2012) *The Reality of ESP: A Physicist's Proof of Psychic Phenomena.* Wheaton, IL: Quest Books, U.S.

Tolle, E. (2001) *The Power of Now: A Guide to Spiritual Enlightenment.* London: Hodder and Stoughton.

Van Praagh, J. (1998) *Talking to Heaven: A Medium's Message of Life after Death.* Wheeler Pub.

Watts, A. (1983) *Myth and Ritual in Christianity.* London: Thames and Hudson.

Watts, A.Y. (1988) *The Book: On the Taboo Against Knowing Who You Are* New York: Vintage Books, [1972, c1966].

Weiss, B. (2001) *Messages from the Masters: Tapping into the Power of Love.* New York: Grand Central Publishing.

Weiss, B.L. and Weiss, M.B.D. (1996) *Many Lives, Many Masters: The True Story of a Prominent Psychiatrist, His Young Patient, and the Past Life Therapy That Changed Both Their Lives.* New York: Grand Central Publishing.

Wikipedia : https://www.wikipedia.org/

Wilcock, D. (2013) *The Synchronicity Key: The Hidden Intelligence Guiding the Universe and You.* New York, NY, United States: Penguin Group (USA).

Zukav, G., Winfrey, O. and Angelou, M. (2014) The Seat of the Soul: 25th *Anniversary Edition.* New York, NY, United States: Simon & Schuster.

https://en.wikiquote.org/wiki/The_Empire_Strikes_Back

LIST OF ILLUSTRATIONS
BY TARA DE FOREST & JANE DE FOREST

ABOUT THE ARTISTS & AUTHOR

© TARA DE FOREST

JANE DE FOREST

ARTIST, INTUITIVE, AUTHOR & TEACHER

KNOWN FOR HER TALENT and integrity as an artist, intuitive coach, animal communicator & medium for more than 20 years.

Jane has painted large-scale murals, commissioned and personal artwork, formal training includes Interlochen Arts Academy and Rhode Island School of Design. Her work and canvases are in collections all over the world from Jane Goodall to Martin Sheen.

In addition to writing, coaching and teaching workshops, Jane also loves to garden, cook and hike with her family in the beautiful northern rainforest of the Pacific Northwest. She's a community volunteer and donates time teaching art in schools; de Forest recently has taken up helping save the bees in her area . In her pro-bono work, she uses ESP to help kids with severe disabilities who can't communicate in traditional way.

"Three generations of women created this work: my elderly mother did the heavy lifting with hours of rewrites, and my 12-year-old art-prodigy daughter Tara illustrated half of it. The romantic image of being a published author dimmed quickly with heated debates (read: editing wars) with my maternal editor about important topics such as commas; this process took three years and seemed to have a mind of its own -- the stories hounded me into the wee hours of the morning when I was without defenses. Once I figured out that writing the stories down insured uninterrupted sleep, this book was born.

I hope this work will make a small difference in a world that has forgotten what is important. I am deeply grateful to my clients and family for allowing me the opportunity to share their private spiritual journeys. Truly, we are all interconnected and entangled . . . love is our foundation . . . I am proud an honored to share my heart with you."   Jane de Forest

TARA DE FOREST

ARTIST

TARA CREATED THE ILLUSTRATIONS for this book when she
was only twelve years old. Growing up surrounded by artists—
Mariah de Forest, her magnificent artist grandmother, as well
as her Grandfather Richard Steinberg, a talented photogra-
pher, and her Godmother artist Christa Grimm and myself
(painter and muralist) — allowed her to absorb creativity
from every direction. In this life her ancestors include such
American artists as: Roy de Forest, Lockwood de Forest
(an associate of Tiffany and president of the Metropolitan
Museum of Art in New York) and George de Forest Brush. But a
past life during the Italian Renaissance could possibly explain
Tara's unschooled ability to accurately duplicate Leonardo Da
Vinci drawings with near perfection . . . at seven years old. Her
mother was stupefied at her raw talent and thrilled that her
talent and ability surpassed all other members of her artistic
family while she was still in grade school. She had her first
one-girl show at Camas Gallery in 2015. Tara likes animals,
waterskiing, ancient history, playing the saxaphone, astrology
and writing.

IN PRAISE OF JANE'S PAINTING

"Jane's work is absolutely lovely. Artists have so much to contribute to our effort of making this a better world, for art speaks to the inner self"

JANE GOODALL, PH.D.
Author of *In the Shadow of Man*
and founder of the Jane Goodall Institute

"Jane certainly does communicate beautifully about the divine mystery that informs all life."

LYNNE TWIST
Author of *The Soul of Money* and founder of Soul Money Institute

"Jane is a true visionary. Her art is a gift of spirit that connects the viewer to the heart of the Sacred. Jane's images are powerful transmissions that can change consciousness and help bring clarity, kindness and compassion into the world".

JOAN BORYSENKO, PH.D.
Author of *A Woman's Journey to God*

© TARA DE FOREST

Jane leads tours to sacred sites.
If you are interested in upcoming trips,
please contact her at
www.janesinspiration.com

30 Day Assignment To Cultivate Your Natural Intuition

© TARA DE FOREST

30 DAY ASSIGNMENT

You must unlearn what you have learned

YODA

1. UNDERSTANDING YOUR INTUITIVE CODE

NOTICE AND DOCUMENT YOUR BODY'S SENSATIONS, feelings and the circumstances in conjunction with those initial intuitive markers. Notice (again). The first step in learning your intuitive code lies in noticing your body's sensations: tingles up the spine, butterflies in your stomach, tightening in your abdomen or a blissful expanded feeling in the top of your head. These sensations are a form of intuitive information, and you, as a living organism, are receiving information all the time. The ability to decipher this information starts with noticing. Just noticing.

Allow yourself to gently notice any colors or images, symbols or feelings of knowing that appear in your physical and internal world throughout your day. By focusing on images instead of words, your logical, left-brain is deemphasized and your intuitive, receptive right-brain is invited to the party, so to speak. Your psychic core is the command center for translating the various symbolic meanings, serendipities, visionary dreams, hunches, and goose bumps (to name a few) that you're receiving.

This psychic core is a pre-verbal, intuitive "Siri" system that operates beyond the multitude of rational human languages. Words limit the potential complexity of this pre-verbal, non-linear communication, and merely point at the meaning of information that contains a multidimensional aspect (such as memory, future foreshadowing, emotion, entire concepts, and mystical understanding).

2. CONNECTING TO THE WEB OF LIGHT

TAKE 20 MINUTES IN MEDITATION or in a quiet contemplative mindset and visualization to imagine yourself connected to a luminous thread that goes from your heart to all those you love, then to all humanity, all animals and all nature. Imagine the luminous thread is made of love and feels like total acceptance and kindness.

Why is this important? It's because accurate intuitive information comes through your right-brain, your so-called gut feeling – NOT your logical brain. In fact, one of my secrets for doing an accurate reading is for me to connect to the web of all life. I use a guided meditation and envision myself as part of everything.

3. PICTURE DRAWING

YOU WILL NEED UNLINED PAPER AND PENCIL, picture cards or photographs.

In this exercise, we will be accessing intuitive information through the process of drawing. Take picture cards or photographs, shuffle them, then randomly pull a card and place it face down in front of you. Hold the pencil loosely, and start by drawing circles and random lines to loosen up your hand. Give yourself a few minutes and allow yourself to draw whatever comes to mind. Once you're done, turn the card over and observe which parts of the card's image you drew accurately.

4. TRAINING YOUR SUBCONSCIOUS

THE MOST IMPORTANT STEP OF ALL. With a red pen, circle your accurate "hits," the times you correctly reproduced the image on the card. There are a number of ways you may get the information correctly: part may be correct; it may be correct but in the incorrect order; or, the color may be correct but the shape is not. Please be merciful with yourself. This takes time. But before long your intuitive core will start to be trained. This intuitive core learns quickly when you acknowledge when it is correct.

5. YOU GOT THIS

ONE OF THE CHARACTERISTICS OF "LIFE ON PLANET EARTH" is that we forget who we really are. It is so easy to forget our greatness and vastness and think we're only our small ego selves. We are taught and culturally conditioned to be limited and separate from each other. These limiting ideas can cause psychic noise in the person attempting to "read" using their sixth sense. By expanding the ideas about who you are and what you are capable of, it becomes easier to realize the vast untapped potential within ourselves.

For private lessons and class on developing & cultivating your natural intuition contact Jane at janesinspiration@gmail.com

"All humans have clairvoyant sensing facilities,
and this is the reason they keep emerging
in spite of any societal resistance to them."

- INGO SWANN,

AUTHOR, ARTIST, VISIONARY, PSYCHONAUT, FATHER OF REMOTE VIEWING

CPSIA information can be obtained
at www.ICGtesting.com
Printed in the USA
FFOW01n0800050418
46131421-47195FF